D1645344

THE
TEN-MINUTE
GARDENER'S
FRUIT-
GROWING
DIARY

www.**transworldbooks**.co.uk

Also by Val Bourne

The Natural Garden
The Winter Garden
Seeds of Wisdom

The Ten-Minute Gardener's Flower-Growing Diary
The Ten-Minute Gardener's Vegetable-Growing Diary

THE
TEN~MINUTE
GARDENER'S
FRUIT~
GROWING
DIARY

Val Bourne

in association with
The Daily Telegraph

BANTAM PRESS

LONDON • TORONTO • SYDNEY • AUCKLAND • JOHANNESBURG

TRANSWORLD PUBLISHERS
61–63 Uxbridge Road, London W5 5SA
A Random House Group Company
www.transworldbooks.co.uk

First published in Great Britain
in 2011 by Bantam Press
an imprint of Transworld Publishers

A CIP catalogue record for this book
is available from the British Library.

ISBN 9780593066706

Addresses for Random House Group Ltd companies outside the UK
can be found at: www.randomhouse.co.uk
The Random House Group Ltd Reg. No. 954009

The Random House Group Limited supports the Forest Stewardship Council (FSC®),
the leading international forest-certification organization. Our books carrying the FSC
label are printed on FSC®-certified paper. FSC is the only forest-certification scheme
endorsed by the leading environmental organizations, including Greenpeace. Our
paper-procurement policy can be found at www.randomhouse.co.uk/environment.

Typeset in Weiss and Mrs Eaves by Falcon Oast Graphic Art Ltd.
Printed and bound in Great Britain by
Clays Limited, Bungay, Suffolk

2 4 6 8 10 9 7 5 3 1

To the Best Beloved, for his helpful marginalia

CONTENTS

ACKNOWLEDGEMENTS

Thank you to Susanna Wadeson for her enthusiastic help and support, without which I would have gone under!

Thank you to Brenda Updegraff for her very necessary, eagle-eyed editing. Thank you to Andrew Davidson for the cover illustration and to Patrick Mulrey for the illustrations inside.

Thank you to Tom Poland and to Philip Lord for the design.

And thank you to my family for their patience over the long months.

PREFACE

GROWING FRUIT appeals to the hedonist in every gardener: after all, what can be better than picking a sun-warmed, perfectly ripe strawberry in June? Once the strawberry crop is over, it's possible to move on to currants and raspberries. Late summer and autumn bring plums, then pears and apples follow, and hopefully a blackberry or two.

It isn't just the flavour. Fruit, especially when it's fresh, is packed full of antioxidants and vitamins. You can control how you grow it, too. It's quite possible to raise fruit organically and this should be everyone's aim in these changing times. Admittedly, you do have to make time to pick it, but once fruit trees and bushes are established they provide the greatest reward of all.

The varieties chosen in this book are the best that plant-breeders can offer and new rootstocks and modern North American breeding are extending our choices. Free-standing apricots and cherries that crop well when young are now a reality, and growing food has never been more popular. So whenever you have a spare 10 minutes, use them wisely because most tasks throughout the year need a little-and-often approach.

Happy gardening.

Val Bourne

JANUARY

This is the month to take a long, hard look at the shape of your fruit trees, for their silhouettes are at their most prominent now. Winter-pruning involves shaping your trees and is never drastic. Apples and pears are pruned when dormant and they can be tackled on clement January days. However, all heavily trained cordons, espaliers and fans are normally shaped towards the end of August when the flow of sap has slowed down (see page 119). Cherries, plums and other stone fruit are pruned in summer, when the rising sap can seal any damage and hopefully prevent diseases from taking hold (see page 110). Take a photograph of these now, however, because it can be very difficult to see their true shape once the leaves appear.

This is also a good month to think about planting fruit trees and bushes. There is still time to put in bare-root fruit bushes, canes and trees before the end of March. Containerized fruit will romp away in spring. Always buy from a fruit specialist: the range is much greater and their expertise is second to none.

1 Plant Fruit Trees
(early January)

ALL FRUIT needs a warm, sunny position that is as sheltered as possible, because most fruit produces a much better crop when cross-pollinated by insects such as bees. The lure is nectar (a sugar-rich energy drink) and the flow is always better in warm conditions. This means that all fruit trees need a position that gets half a day's sunshine – preferably in the afternoon. Given this, the bees will visit.

Frost pockets make poor positions for fruit because blossom is inevitably browned and ruined. Observe your plot, identify the areas where frost lurks the longest and avoid using these parts. If your garden is cold (as mine is), opt for later-flowering varieties. Ideally your trees, bushes or plants should be sheltered from strong winds. Commercial orchards often use deciduous trees like willow, alder and poplar as shelter belts. Gardeners usually plant a biddable hedge (not a fast conifer hedge) or erect a fence.

The soil needs to be well drained – heavy, waterlogged soil is not good for fruit. Planting on a slope encourages better drainage, but if you are on low-lying land you may want to consider a drainage system or you could incorporate lots of grit. Most gardeners, however, can achieve good drainage by adding extra organic matter when planting. A yearly mulch also helps (see page 17).

Fruit trees are virtually permanent features of the productive garden, so it's well worth getting the planting right. You can plant in February if it is mild enough, and in March before bud break; but October and November are the best months for planting. December is possible if the weather remains mild.

After you have chosen your site, the first job is to clear the ground of perennial weeds. It is best to hand-weed carefully while preparing the ground. Try not to use herbicide – but if you do, take care to choose one that will not damage your tree. Double digging is best as it gives roots extra depth and is especially useful where the subsoil is difficult and needs disturbing – see page 155. The addition of well-rotted compost or manure will not only improve drainage (see above) but will dramatically improve the soil structure.

This work can be done some time in advance, but just before planting fork in a general fertilizer such as blood, fish and bone at the recommended rate.

Do not plant if the soil is very cold. You will need to keep the tree somewhere frost-free, like a shed, until it warms up. Trees come either in a pot or bare-rooted. Generally, it is better to buy bare-rooted specimens because they adapt better to your soil conditions – for concise tips on how to plant them, see page 141.

Dig a hole wide enough to take the roots of your tree fully spread out. Mound the soil up slightly in the middle. Make sure that you plant the tree to the same depth as before, which should be visible as a mark on the stem. If you can't see it, make sure that the graft scar, if there is one, is about 10cm (4in) above the finished soil surface. Back-fill the hole, working the soil into any gaps, and finally firm and level the soil. Stake straight after planting, making sure that the trunk is about 8cm (3in) from the stake. Add a mulch of 5–8cm (2–3in) of compost or manure if the ground is warm enough (see page 17). Fasten the stem to the stake using a soft tie, then water well.

If you're serious about soft fruit you will need a good fruit cage to keep the birds away. Redcurrants, raspberries and blueberries are top targets – and who can blame them? Fruit cages are not cheap, but you will recoup the cost relatively quickly because fruit is so expensive to buy. If a metal one is out of the question due to price, improvise and build a wooden one.

Did you know? Fruit varieties are often over 100 years old and many are local to a particular area. In many cases they have adapted to local conditions like poor soil, a windy location or cold weather. Research your local varieties by consulting a specialist nursery, because regionality is really important when it comes to apples and pears. Local apple groups and Common Ground (www.commonground.org.uk/01747 850820) will advise you.

SECRETS OF SUCCESS

- Research thoroughly. Look round the gardens in your local area to see what types of fruit grow well.
- Explore varieties and choose those that suit your site. Select the correct rootstock (see page 109) to go with the variety.
- Take into account flowering times and self-incompatibility when selecting varieties (see page 59).
- Prepare the soil well when planting all fruit.
- Feed regularly as appropriate.

2 Winter-prune Gooseberries
(early January)

GOOSEBERRIES may be savage, prickly beasts, but they provide the first fresh fruit of the year for many gardeners. Culinary varieties can be cooked alone, or added to mixed fruit compôtes. Some dessert varieties can be eaten raw, but unfortunately their distinctive muscat flavour is adored by blackbirds. You can buy standards (bushes grafted on to a tall single stem) or bushes; both produce a large amount of fruit – up to 5kg (11lb) per bush in some cases.

Gooseberries are very versatile. They are self-fertile, so one bush can be grown alone, which is an advantage in a small garden. Gooseberry bushes can also do well in partial shade and they withstand harsh conditions, of both temperature and wind, which makes them a good choice for cooler areas – though if you have a windy garden you should probably avoid standards, as they can snap under the weight of fruit in summer gales. Standards do fit well into flower borders, however, and this is one fruit bush that is extremely long-lived.

In winter cut back the leading stems by half. The side shoots (or laterals) are cut back to two buds. This encourages fruiting spurs to form on the old wood. Once this has been done, check that the framework of the bush is open enough and remove more wood if the crown seems congested. An open middle makes picking easier.

Did you know? Lancashire weavers were a competitive bunch and by the 1740s they were holding gooseberry shows where the biggest and best won. By 1815 there were 120 of these shows in the north of England. The largest yellow gooseberry, exhibited in Stockport in 1830, was named 'The Teaser'. The largest red, from Nantwich, was dubbed 'Roaring Lion' and the largest white, from Ormskirk, was 'Ostrich'. Darwin wrote about their 2oz fruits and many varieties still grown today date from this competitive era.

Organic Tip ✔

Mildew is a disease of drought-stressed plants and can be a problem with gooseberries, especially on light soil or in drier areas. American gooseberry mildew arrived in the UK in the early 1900s and devastated the gooseberry industry. However, if mildew does strike, it isn't fatal and modern varieties have been bred for resistance. If you are on the eastern, drier side of Britain, or if your soil is light, always opt for a modern variety and mulch in summer.

SECRETS OF SUCCESS WITH GOOSEBERRIES

- These versatile plants are easy to grow and they thrive all over Britain in a variety of soils and situations, including cold gardens and semi-shade.
- The culinary varieties are too sour to tempt the birds, but the dessert varieties come under concentrated attack in July. These will need netting.
- Dig in 5cm (2in) well-rotted manure or garden compost over the whole area before planting.
- Plant each bush 1.5m (5ft) apart during the dormant season (November–February).
- Stake half-standards well and tie them in using soft ties.
- If you are trying to produce large dessert gooseberries to eat, thin the fruit in May by removing every other berry. The thinnings can be cooked.

'Invicta' AGM

This recent, vigorous culinary variety is immune to American gooseberry mildew. It yields very highly. Pick in late July and allow 1.8m (6ft) between each bush.

'Hinnomaki Yellow'

This dessert variety produces large, yellow fruit similar to the popular old but mildew-prone variety 'Leveller'. Pick in mid-July. It is one of a Finnish-bred series, so is very hardy.

'Pax'

A virtually spineless, upright gooseberry with large, plum-red berries that can be cooked or eaten. Mildew resistance is very high. Pick in July.

'Whinham's Industry'

This dark-red, hairy gooseberry has a superb, very sweet flavour and makes wonderful jam. Raised by Mr Whinham of Morpeth before 1850, it produces a remarkable crop.

3 Winter-prune Apples
(mid-January)

NOW IS the time to winter-prune your dormant apple trees using sharp secateurs and a pruning saw. Winter-pruning should be a gentle affair carried out in clement conditions, not in really cold or unpleasant weather. Remove the 3 Ds – dead, diseased or dying wood. Then take out any branches that cross and any that are too close to the ground. The aim is to produce an open-centred tree, but remember that the more you prune, the more the tree will try to replace the leafy growth it has lost and the less fruit it will produce. Varieties vary greatly in habit and bud formation, but try to encourage branches to develop horizontally and cut out those that rise up steeply. More fruit buds are formed when the sap is running more slowly. All cuts should be made just above an outward-facing bud, if possible, to encourage a spreading habit.

How you prune will depend on the maturity of the tree,

but all winter pruning should aim to preserve the fruit buds. These are fatter and rounder than the pointed leafy buds and it should be possible to spot them on short, knobbly spurs and on the year-old wood of lateral branches. The object is to preserve these and encourage more spurs and laterals to develop. Be aware, though, that a few apple varieties are tip-bearing (with apples forming on the ends of shoots). With these, all the unprofitable wood should be removed and the laterals should be shortened to four–six buds.

Did you know? Until recently it was thought that apples had evolved from the wild crab apples found in the English countryside. However, new genetic research has revealed that our apple varieties began life in the fruit forests of the Tien Shan in central Asia. Initially seeds were spread by bears and birds, but travellers and their pack animals also ate the fruit and so spread the seeds beyond their native region.

VARIETIES

'Lord Lambourne' AGM
A compact dessert apple that's excellent in a small garden. Aromatic flavour and good Cox colour. Pick in mid-autumn and store until late autumn. Pollination Group B.

'Egremont Russet' AGM
Honey-coloured, rough skin and grainy flesh with a distinctive nutty flavour. Pick in mid-autumn and store until late autumn. Pollination Group B.

For further varieties of apple, see September, pages 129 and 133.

SECRETS OF SUCCESS

- Aim to end up with an airy shape that simplifies the silhouette. Try to achieve a goblet shape with about five main branches.
- Teach yourself to recognize fruit buds as opposed to leaf buds.
- Gentle pruning encourages gentle growth and that will encourage fruit buds.
- Hard pruning provokes a quick reaction. In fruit this means lots of slender, fast-growing shoots that bear leaves but not fruit.
- Growth is controlled by rootstock. Dwarf rootstocks need light pruning. See page 121.
- Some varieties, such as 'Rev. Wilks' (an excellent early cooker), have exceptionally spreading habits, so the pruning of young trees should be to inside and not outside buds as is usual.

4 Winter-prune Pears
(mid-January)

PEARS PREFER warmth, so are generally less suited to the cool British climate than apples. Certain warmer areas of Britain, often close to rivers, do suit them, however, and Waterperry in

Oxfordshire has the name to prove it. It isn't just a north–south divide, though. The area round Jedburgh in south-east Scotland was at one time a renowned pear-growing district. However, growing pears in some British gardens can be difficult and this is why pear trees were often planted on warm walls in centuries past. Warmth is also needed for the growth of the pollen tube before fruit can be formed (see page 59), so a cool early summer can affect the crop. Pears usually give lower yields than apples and they do not store as reliably either.

Many pears form upright, goblet-shaped trees with a narrow arrangement of tall branches. Winter pruning will keep the shape open and the leaders can be tipped back every winter. These upright branches can be cut diagonally down from left to right in one year and then from right to left in the following year to balance the shoots and keep the leader straighter. The laterals and side shoots are shortened, as they are for apples, to four–six buds.

Quince is used as a rootstock for pears because they are closely related, and as a result they are thirsty. There are two types: Quince A rootstock, which is vigorous, produces trees that reach up to 3–9m (12–19ft) or more, while the less vigorous Quince C trees reach up to 3m (10ft) after 5 years. Fruit-growers graft vigorous varieties on to Quince C to slow their development, while less vigorous varieties are grafted on to Quince A to boost their growth.

Quince C is suited to wetter soil, but Quince A is the most widely available. (For more on rootstocks, see page 109.)

Did you know? By the twelfth century pears were being imported from France and many of today's pear varieties have French names like 'Glou Morceau'. Over time, texture changed from gritty pears that often needed cooking (like 'Doyenne du Comice') to better-textured pears that were delicious eaten fresh. However, in 1885 a new pear called 'Conference' was bred by the Rivers nursery in Sawbridgeworth and it soon became the most successful commercial variety in Britain.

Organic Tip ✔

Pears are naturally very deep-rooted and this balances their tall physique. However, because they are grafted on to quince rootstocks, which are shallow-rooted, this makes them vulnerable to being rocked by the wind when in leaf. Therefore pear trees need staking for at least 5 years — much longer than apples.

SECRETS OF SUCCESS

- Pear blossom opens earlier than apple blossom and is more likely to get frosted, so choose a warm position in the most frost-free place you have.
- If your garden is cold or frost-prone, opt for a later-flowering variety. Cold temperatures and pear production do not go together.
- Choose a good variety from a specialist.
- Stake for 5 years.
- Take time and trouble when pruning in winter.

VARIETIES

'Doyenne du Comice' AGM

The classic, grainy-textured pear for cooking – a plump, round, pale-skinned delight. Needs a warm position. Pick mid-autumn and store until early winter. Scab can be a problem. Pollination Group C.

'Conference' AGM

The most reliable pear of all, producing slender fruit for eating rather than cooking. Pick when firm in early autumn and allow to ripen. Keeps for 4 weeks. Self-fertile, but fruits best when cross-pollinated. Pollination Group B.

'Concorde' AGM

A British-bred, self-fertile hybrid between 'Conference' and 'Doyenne du Comice', bearing heavy crops of medium-sized, rounded fruits on a compact tree. Pick in late October. Pollination Group C.

'Beth' AGM

A new English-bred variety that comes into fruit early and regularly. The white flesh has a melting texture and yields are high. Pick in late August. Pollination Group D.

For further varieties of pear, see September, page 130.

5 Renovate Old Fruit Trees
(late January)

IF YOU HAVE inherited an old fruit tree and it's cropping well, leave it alone. However, if it's in a bad condition but you enjoy the fruit, it may be worth taking the time and trouble to rejuvenate it. To lessen the shock, this should be tackled over 4–5 years rather than all in one go. If the experiment fails, console yourself with the fact that fruit wood makes wonderful logs.

The project is often more viable with an apple or pear tree than with a stone fruit tree, but if you love your tree, do fight for it. Tackle one quarter per year during clement winter weather. Aim to simplify the shape so that the canopy is open, allowing air to circulate. A shaded middle is bad news. Shade prevents the initiation of fruit buds because the wood doesn't get chance to ripen in the sun: it tends to become limp and etiolated instead. Any fruit produced is likely to lack flavour too because the sun can't ripen it. Good light is also vital for sweet fruit.

Start by removing all dead, diseased and dying wood, then cut away any crossing branches right across the tree. This will simplify the shape and allow you a better view. Examine a quarter of the tree from afar and decide where to make the cuts that will improve the shape. Large limbs may need removing and you may have to cut them away in sections. You will need to make undercuts (from the bottom of the branch) first before sawing downwards so that you get a clean cut. Aim to saw back to where the branch you are removing joins a larger branch. Try to cut it almost flush, but leave a stub to callous over. Do not leave a stump.

SECRETS OF SUCCESS

- Treat every tree as an individual.
- Be safe. Invest in a good stepladder or platform.
- Start by winter-pruning and tidying the entire tree,
  then assess the shape of one quarter before radically
  pruning it, one quarter per year.
- Use sharp tools and make undercuts before sawing
  downwards.
- Take your time and get down to the ground regularly
  between cuts to assess the shape of your tree.
- Don't leave stumps — they will die back and cause fungal
  diseases.
- Tidy up thoroughly afterwards.

Did you know? The original 'Bramley Seedling' still survives in Church Street, Southwell, Nottingham more than 200 years after Mary Ann Brailsford planted a pip in her parents' garden at some point between 1809 and 1813 when she left to get married. In 1846 the house was bought by a butcher named Matthew Bramley. In 1856 the tree came to the attention of a local nurseryman, Henry Merryweather, who asked if he could take cuttings. Matthew Bramley agreed but insisted that the cooking apple should be named after him. The first trees descended from it were sold in 1862. In 1900 a severe storm blew down the original Bramley apple tree, but it was restored to health and still bears apples today.

Organic Tip ✔

Bear in mind that the majority of fruit trees are most productive up to 25 years of age, so a tree older than this will never be as bountiful as a youngster. On the plus side, a mature, gnarled fruit tree is an amazing sculptural feature and supports a lot of wildlife.

6 Mulch and Feed Fruit Trees
(late January)

MULCHING any plant has to be carefully timed because the ground must be moist and reasonably warm; otherwise you could trap frost into the soil for some months. Towards the end of January winter often begins to loosen its grip and mulching now will retain moisture in spring and suppress weeds. Both will help your fruit trees, bushes and canes greatly. Care must be taken to keep the mulch away from the trunks of trees, however.

Over time, a mulch of organic matter will be pulled down into the ground by worms and this will improve the soil structure and aid drainage. The very best material for mulching fruit trees is well-rotted animal manure – this should smell sweet, without any hint of ammonia. Source it carefully: some gardeners have had problems with manure contaminated by a persistent hormone weedkiller called aminopyralid (see page 190). For this reason, many people have turned to using their own garden compost instead.

Some gardeners prefer decorative mulches like bark, especially if their fruit trees are in the garden. All mulches rot down on the soil's surface, using up nitrogen in the process. If the material is low in nutrients (like bark, for instance), you need to replace lost nitrogen by sprinkling on a nitrogen-rich feed before mulching. Powdered chicken manure (sold as 6X) is light to handle and an excellent plant food for leafy growth. A further application of fertilizer in March is also useful.

Did you know? Garden soils generally contain high levels of phosphate, so bonemeal should be used only every 3 years. Apply 100–125g per square metre (3–4oz per square yard).

Organic Tip ✔

Blackcurrants, pears and plums need more nitrogen than other fruits and these should be given a nitrogen feed every March: 100g per square metre (3oz per square yard) is ideal.

SECRETS OF SUCCESS

- Try to use organic fertilizers. They improve soil structure as well as adding nutrients. They include manure, slurry, seaweed, guano, compost and bonemeal.
- Liquid seaweed seems to cure most deficiencies and it helps fruit to resist pests like red spider mite, aphids and fungal infections.
- Always follow the instructions on fertilizer packets to the letter. Weigh it to ensure you use the right quantity.

SOIL REQUIREMENTS

Nitrogen

This promotes leafy growth rather than flower. As a result, crops like strawberries, raspberries and apples do not benefit from too much nitrogen.

Potash

This is essential for fruit colour and flavour, for flower-bud development and for hardening the wood to prevent frost damage. Red-edged leaves indicate a shortage. It should be applied once a year in spring. Use sulphate of potash or seaweed meal as directed. Crops like strawberries need a high-potash feed every 2 weeks during the growing season. Tomato food has just the right proportion of nutrients for fruiting and flowering plants. This is watered on.

Magnesium

This is usually deficient only in sandy soils. The biggest clue is early leaf fall. Epsom salts can be applied: 33g per square metre (1oz per square yard).

Iron

Alkaline soil is often short of available iron and raspberries are prone to iron-deficiency, which causes them to develop yellowing foliage. Use a water-on iron supplement, or mulch heavily to reduce soil pH, so that any iron in the soil then becomes available.

FEBRUARY

*A*t the moment the garden hovers between winter and spring, which seem to be battling it out on a daily basis. Although everyone longs for spring, for that moment when the jacket can be shrugged off with confidence, the experienced gardener secretly prays that winter keeps a firm grip until mid-March. Precocious springs tend to fade and the weather seesaws back and forth with serious consequences for fruit-growers. It's much better if the buds stay firmly closed in February.

Fruit trees, bushes and canes should look meticulously tidy, like well-trained soldiers standing to attention. Check supports and ties. If you're thinking of planting, bare-root trees or bushes (if you can find them at this late stage) could still be planted now and this is one of the best months for establishing containerized fruit, which can be grown in pots as well as in the ground.

1 Cut Back Autumn-fruiting Raspberries

(early February)

AUTUMN raspberries crop, on average, from mid-August until early November, if the weather holds, on this year's new canes. This is the best time to cut the canes back. I prefer to reduce them all to ground level; however, some gardeners leave half the canes up and take half of them out so that they get June–July fruit on the uncut canes. This seems unnecessarily complicated – I prefer to grow summer-fruiting raspberries to pre-empt the autumn ones (see page 53). I also feel that cutting down completely now promotes stronger growth in spring, producing more vigorous canes.

The time to prune summer raspberries is after fruiting. Now, they should only be 'tipped back' – just remove the top 15cm (6in), where buds tend to be of a poor quality.

Collect up all the prunings carefully and either shred them or cut them up finely for the compost heap. Check all the ties and supports, making repairs as necessary. After pruning, dig lightly through the soil to disturb any overwintering raspberry beetles. If you have chickens, get them to help.

Did you know? Raspberries contain lots of vitamin C, plus other antioxidants, flavonoids and potassium. They are delicious eaten raw, they can be made into jam in less than 5 minutes (if the fruit is very fresh) and they also freeze better than any other soft fruit. Children love them.

Organic Tip ✔

Autumn-fruiting raspberries are the easier of the two to grow because their sturdy canes do not need staking as those of summer-fruiting varieties do. They are also less affected by raspberry beetle, which is more active when the summer varieties are fruiting. They do well in drier gardens as long as they are mulched because they fruit in cooler conditions — something raspberries enjoy. Water well in dry August weather.

SECRETS OF SUCCESS

- Raspberries tend to wander away from the row, so they need firm control. Chop out any unwanted canes in early spring just as they appear.
- Keep rows of raspberry canes weeded and give them an annual feed in late winter. Mulch with well-rotted manure.
- Don't thin within the row unless they are very crowded, and then only take out the weakest ones.

VARIETIES OF AUTUMN-FRUITING RASPBERRY

'Autumn Bliss' AGM
Firm, well-flavoured fruit that starts to ripen in August and carries on until late in the year.

'Polka'
The earliest of the autumn-fruiting raspberries. Very aromatic and high-yielding with a clean, fruity flavour. A possible replacement for 'Autumn Bliss'.

'Joan J'
A new, almost spine-free variety producing large red berries.

'Fallgold'
A yellow raspberry with a sweet flavour.

For varieties of summer-fruiting raspberry, see March, page 53.

2 Feed Your Strawberries
(early February)

AT THIS time of year strawberries can look very battered by the winter. If the weather is reasonable, tidy your plants lightly by cutting dead and damaged leaves away and then give them their first feed of the year, but try to wait for the worst of winter to pass. A potash-rich fertilizer will boost flower and fruit growth. Avoid nitrogen-rich feeds now; they will promote too much leafy growth. There are sprinkle-on granular feeds for strawberries, but liquid tomato food or comfrey tea (see page 163) work just as well.

As spring progresses, continue to tidy your plants and give the plot a weed. If flowers appear early, it's vital to prevent frost from blackening them. Cover them with hessian or horticultural fleece on cool nights.

Did you know? The strawberry we grow today is a descendant of an accidental eighteenth-century hybrid between a Chilean strawberry, *Fragaria chiloense*, and a North American species, *F. virginiana*. Antoine Nicolas Duchesne, botanist and gardener at the Palace of Versailles, grew both and, when planted side by side, they hybridized to produce large red fruit. The same hybrids were deliberately bred in England in the late eighteenth century by Thomas Andrew Knight, a horticulturalist and botanist who lived at Downton Castle in Herefordshire, and Michael Keen, a nurseryman of Isleworth in London, both of whom raised and named early varieties.

Organic Tip ✔

Strawberries are members of the rose family and, just like roses, suffer from 'rose-sickness' — a debilitating condition whereby roses planted in ground that has recently held other roses do not thrive. If you want to replace a wintertime fatality in an existing strawberry bed you will need to replace the old soil with fresh soil in which strawberries have not been grown.

SECRETS OF SUCCESS

- There are three types of strawberry plant: cold-stored plants are available between March and June; misted-tip plants (grown from cuttings) can be bought in August (see page 117); and freshly dug plants are available during October. Plant all as soon as they arrive.
- You must conduct a war on three fronts in order to grow strawberries successfully: against disease, slugs and birds. Tidiness and regular care are important.
- Cut away dead and damaged leaves close to the crowns. Do not try to pull them off – you will damage the crown.
- If you have missed any runners, remove them now.
- Do not add bulky organic matter as a substitute for liquid feeds – it encourages slugs.
- Rotate your crop and discard plants once they are 4–5 years old. Avoid planting where potatoes have grown before or they will be at risk from verticillium wilt. Do not plant potatoes close to a strawberry bed for the same reason.

'Honeoye' AGM (early)
A good flavour with conical, orange-red, glossy berries. Good in cool districts.

'Sonata' (mid-season)
Large, sweet fruit that resists extreme weather, including very hot spells and heavy rain. Resistant to powdery mildew.

'Hapil' AGM (mid-season)
Heavy crops of large, bright-red, glossy berries with an excellent sweet flavour. Crops especially well on light soils and in drier conditions.

'Fenella' (late)
Heavy-yielding with large, glossy berries that have an aromatic, sweet flavour. Good resistance to verticillium wilt and crown rot, and the fruit can tolerate very heavy rain.

'Florence' AGM
Disease-resistant, heavy-cropping strawberry with large, dark red fruits with a very good flavour. Shows some resistance to vine weevil.

For further varieties of strawberry, see March, page 38.

3 Plant and Train Blackberries
(mid-February)

IF YOU haven't grown a cultivated blackberry, it's well worth doing so. The flowers appear after the frosts have stopped, so they make good productive plants for cold gardens or those in frost pockets. They can be trained in a corner of the garden as long as they are given the support of a wall or fence and allowed to climb into a brighter position. They are not fussy about soil, even seeming to tolerate heavy soil. Given a reasonable position, they can produce over 5kg (10lb) of fruit per plant.

Choose the variety to fit the space available. Some need as little as 2m (6ft); others, such as 'Fantasia', need 4.5m (15ft). Hybrid varieties are generally smaller. Blackberries can be planted any time in the dormant season, November–March. Dig in 5–8cm (2–3in) of well-rotted compost or manure thoroughly at the planting site.

The key to growing cultivated blackberries successfully lies in pruning and training. Blackberries fruit on last year's canes from late summer until the first frosts. Next year's canes sprout from the rootstock from midsummer on and their vigorous growth gets in the way of picking if they are not contained.

The answer is to train the new canes away from the old canes. The easiest way is to train all canes one way on the supporting wire frame one year and the other way the next. This one-way system is wasteful of space, however, since only half the frame is productive in any one year.

A second way is to train the new canes vertically, having already trained last year's canes well to the left and right to leave a gap for them. The new canes are gradually gathered together into a tight bundle which is fixed to the frame. The old canes are cut away after fruiting and the bundle of new canes is left in place over winter.

Now is the time to train the new canes into their fruiting positions. Undo the bundle and tie in the flexible canes horizontally to the frame. If the canes are long they can be woven up and down.

Dig over the soil underneath the canes to uncover any pests. With luck the birds will eat any overwintering raspberry beetles; these also attack blackberries. Then top-dress the area with a general fertilizer.

Did you know? In medieval England it was widely believed that the devil spat or urinated on all the blackberries in the hedgerows on Michaelmas Day, 29 September, so countrydwellers eschewed them after that date. Late fruit does tend to ferment, giving it a strange flavour.

Organic Tip ✔

Blackberries like warm sunshine and they grow best along the Pacific coast of Oregon. Try to train yours into positions where the branches pick up afternoon sunshine even if the roots are in shade.

SECRETS OF SUCCESS

- Space plants in rows 1.8m (6ft) apart if growing more than one.
- Erect wire frames to support the branches and make picking easier. These should be in place prior to planting.
- Train the canes horizontally: they will produce much more fruit.
- Cut out the old fruiting canes after flowering to promote vigour.
- Keep the area around blackberries well weeded.

VARIETIES

'Bedford Giant'
An early-fruiting variety producing large clusters of flavourful, round berries from late July to August. A very vigorous variety – not suitable for a small garden.

'Karaka Black'
A new, very early variety from New Zealand. This 'King' blackberry produces elongated fruit by July and carries on for 2 months. The fruit is easy to pick.

'Loch Ness'
This thornless blackberry produces very high yields of top-quality fruit. Berries are large, very firm and glossy black. The most successful commercial variety in Britain.

'Oregon'
A thornless blackberry with divided leaves that crops in late August or September. Can be safely planted against a wall or fence as it has smooth stems. A lighter cropper.

4 Prune Newly Planted Plums

(mid-February)

PLUMS MAKE excellent fruit trees for small gardens because many varieties are self-fertile – so you can plant one tree and get a crop. The golden rule is that you never prune plums in winter because of the risk of silver leaf disease. The time to prune established trees throughout their productive life is in the second half of July (see page 110). However, newly planted plum trees will need pruning just as the buds are breaking for the first 2 years.

In the first year cut the main leader (the branch forming the apex of the tree) back to 1.5m (5ft). Then shorten the laterals by half. Any branches that are too close to the ground should be removed at their source. Prune again in late July – then in the following March the only pruning that is required is to tip back the main leader by two-thirds.

Did you know? Plums have been grown in the Vale of Evesham for hundreds of years. One authority, Ron Sidwell (1909–93), who spent his life studying their requirements and eventually became vice principal of Pershore College, was famous for being able to name every plum variety from its stone alone. He mapped the weather all over the region to discover the most frost-free area for commercial plum-growing, finally identifying a hamlet called Little Paris on Bredon Hill as the most frost-free spot. He moved there and established a large, fruitful garden, Bredon Springs, containing many frost-tender plants from the southern hemisphere. Sidwell went on to breed the famous Bird Series of penstemons, including 'Raven', 'Blackbird' and 'Osprey', resurrecting the penstemon's popularity once again in the 1960s.

Organic Tip ✔

The fungus that causes silver leaf is closely related to wood-decomposing fungi. Like them, it fruits on wood from late summer on and can survive for a long time in cut wood. So infected branches can be cut away during the summer without any risk of spreading the disease, but all wood and leaves should be burned to kill the fungus.

SECRETS OF SUCCESS WITH PLUMS

- Plums (like all stone fruits) flower early in the year and need to be planted in areas that escape spring frosts. They also need a sheltered position to encourage pollinators. Gages need a warm position and can be difficult to grow in cold districts.
- Plums prefer well-drained, moisture-retentive soil and do best in areas where summer rainfall tends to be plentiful.
- Mulch with well-rotted manure in mid-spring to preserve moisture and increase nitrogen (see page 17). Top-dress with potash-rich fertilizer in late winter.
- Plum trees can be wayward in shape, so branches may need tying down, raising up or trimming back during the growing season.
- Branches can snap under the weight of fruit, so thin out the crop if this looks likely.
- Pick some plums with the stalk attached a little before they become fully ripe: this way they will keep for 3 weeks in a cool place.
- Remove any mummified plums in the autumn — these will harbour brown rot spores over winter and cause re-infection the following year.

'Opal' AGM

A new, extra-early variety with medium-sized, yellow-fleshed, red fruits. Very good to eat, but also makes good jam. Pick in late July. Self-fertile. Pollination Group C.

'Czar' AGM

A dark, purple-black plum for cooking and jam but it can also be eaten raw when fully ripe. Yellow–green flesh with a good acid flavour. Pick in early August. Reliable and seems to shrug off frost. Self-fertile. Pollination Group C.

'Marjorie's Seedling' AGM

The best late plum for cooking and eating, although it forms a large tree. It flowers later than most and the blossom appears after the leaves (which is unusual), so it misses the early frosts. Pick in late September. Self-fertile. Pollination Group B.

'Victoria' AGM

The most popular plum with both amateur and commercial growers because it crops reliably year after year. Yellowish-green flesh and a pink-bloomed skin, but the wood is brittle. Pick in mid-August. Self-fertile. Pollination Group C.

5 Prune Cobnuts and Filberts
(late February)

BY LATE February the hazel catkins will be sending up clouds of yellow pollen. This is the traditional time to prune the trees, so that the magic yellow dust (the male pollen) falls on to the small red female flowers, which resemble tiny sea anemones.

The ideal nut tree should be a multi-stemmed bush, roughly 1.5–2m (5–6ft) in height for easy pruning and picking. Prune between January and March, aiming to create a bowl shape with an open centre containing eight or so branches radiating from a central stem. Pruning is simple: you saw some of the older, thicker branches out at the base. If this is one now, while they are devoid of leaf, these strong pieces of wood can be used as bean poles or pea sticks, depending on their size. Growing hazels is a sustainable system, providing both nuts and staking material.

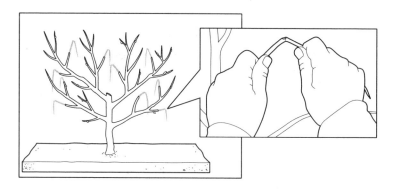

In late summer the newer shoots will look like narrow whips. Bend the upper half over (leaving it attached) to slow the sap. This will encourage more flower buds. In autumn the warm-brown nuts will nestle in a lighter green ruff. The time to harvest is when those ruffs turn yellow. Unfortunately the squirrels often beat the gardener to the crop.

Nutteries can be very decorative because they make an ideal canopy for all manner of woodlanders including hellebores, snowdrops and spring bulbs. So your nut trees can be incorporated into an ornamental garden – unless you have room for a nuttery like Sissinghurst's (see page 123). If you do, so much the better – hazel wood is the best for staking plants.

Organic Tip ✔

Dig and weed the ground under nut trees during winter. This should expose the larvae of the nut weevil, a troublesome pest, to the winter frosts.

Did you know? The name 'hazel' comes from the Anglo-Saxon word *haesel* meaning a head-dress or bonnet, referring to the shape of the outer husk. Cobnuts and filberts come from different species of hazel. Cobnuts (*Corylus avellana*) are bred from our native hazel and produce round nuts with a short husk. Filberts come from a south-eastern European species called *Corylus maxima* and the nuts are longer, with a pointed top and long husks. They take their common name from St Philbert, whose feast day is 20 August, when picking starts.

SECRETS OF SUCCESS WITH HAZELNUTS

- Plant in a sunny, open position where the hazel can expand as a specimen tree. Leave 3m (10ft) between trees if possible. Keep young trees well watered in their first three growing seasons.
- Cobnuts dislike heavy, waterlogged clay. They do well in poor, well-drained sandy loams, such as parts of Kent, where 'plats' (cobnut orchards) have always been commercially successful. A soil that is too fertile will tend to produce vigorous trees that don't crop well.
- Young branches should be trained to near horizontal (a hoop can be used) and the lateral spread is encouraged by always pruning to just above an outward-facing bud.
- Propagate cobnuts by bending established suckers over and pegging them down.

6 Prepare Fruit-cage Netting and Fleece

(late February)

FEBRUARY is a quiet month in the fruit garden once winter-pruning has finished, so it is an ideal time to check over the fruit-cage netting. If you took the top cover off to prevent snow from bending the uprights, reinstate it now. Take at least one side panel off to allow larger bees to access the fruit flowers, or choose a larger mesh to allow them in. Although fruit is often self-fertile, crops are normally higher if plants are cross-pollinated.

Strawberries may flower as early as April in warm springs, but they are very susceptible to frost. Be prepared to fleece the flowers on cold evenings with hessian or heavyweight horticultural fleece. Use bricks or stone as weights if it is likely to be windy. Peaches and apricots will need fleecing too.

Did you know? Nets have been used to protect fruit since Roman times at least. The writer and farmer Columella (AD 4–70) describes nets made of broom being used to prevent birds from eating pomegranates. The diarist John Evelyn describes using nets in 1686, but the earliest wire fruit cage was a nineteenth-century invention designed to prevent birds from eating cherries.

Organic Tip ✔

If you do fleece strawberries and other fruit, remember to remove the blanket every morning to allow pollinators access to the flowers.

SECRETS OF SUCCESS WITH NETTING

- Pick the right mesh size for the job.
- Treat mesh gently – undesirables will find even the smallest hole.
- If you can, add a small (10–15cm/4–6in) protective wooden plinth around the foot of the fruit cage. A plinth made from rustic planking – 'edged slabwood' in the trade – looks good too.
- Take the roof netting off in winter. Many fruit cages are destroyed by the weight of snow.

MARCH

March is an excellent time to plant fruit, just as the soil begins to warm up in the strengthening sun. The bare-root season is really over by now, but container-grown fruit trees, bushes and plants will romp away at this time of year. Order this month (using a specialist supplier) and work on preparing the soil so that you can plant them as soon as they arrive. Double dig the areas where planting is to take place and add organic material – well-rotted manure or matter from the compost heap.

This is also a good time to get rid of fruit that isn't performing. Strawberries, for instance, lose vigour after 4–5 years and need to be replaced by new plants, and you may have found that a particular apple doesn't do well for you. If you are removing any fruit, do not replant the same crop in the same spot. Give it a fresh site, as the soil may either harbour diseases or be exhausted.

1 Make a New Strawberry Bed
(early March)

MOST PLANTINGS of fruit are semi-permanent: once in position they stay there for decades. Strawberries, however, are moveable feasts that inhabit the same spot for 5 years at most; after that their productivity plummets and they need replacing. For this reason they are often best incorporated in the vegetable garden, although they must never rub shoulders with potatoes or tomatoes as they share a disease – verticillium wilt.

Strawberries are traditionally planted 37–45cm (15–18in) apart in rows 90cm (3ft) apart. This allows enough space for hoeing between plants. It also allows you to water without damaging and splashing the fruit. They can, though, be grown very successfully in small (2.4 × 1.2m/8 × 4ft) beds. The plants and rows are spaced more closely, at 30cm (12in). Eighteen plants in such a bed will give you 13kg (30lb) of fruit over a 5-week period.

Choose a warm, sunny position and try to give your plants good drainage and good soil. Avoid a frost pocket; the crop will be ruined if frost catches the flowers. Before planting, incorporate plenty of bulky organic matter. Two barrowloads on a 2.4 × 1.2m (8 × 4ft) bed will be ample. Be sure to pick out any perennial weeds, as it is impossible to remove them once the bed is established.

Take care when planting. Trim back the roots to roughly 10cm (4in), then spread them out in the hole. Ensure that the base of the crown rests lightly on the surface. Planting at the correct depth is important: if the crown is planted too deeply it will rot; if it is planted too shallowly the plants will dry out and die.

It is often a good idea to begin a new strawberry bed whilst the old one is 3 or 4 years old – so that there isn't a gap in production. When making a new bed it's best to order in fresh plants that are guaranteed virus-free. Strawberries are very susceptible to virus and you must always buy certified virus-free plants: do not accept next door's freebies, however tempting they may be. Breeders constantly launch new varieties, so be adaptable about which to grow. The home gardener is always advised to scrap their plants every 4–5 years and start again. This makes sound sense.

There are three types of plants on offer in the nursery trade. The conventional plants raised from runners are sent out in early autumn. These will flower in the following summer, but all flowers formed this year should be removed to allow the plant to concentrate on producing a good root system. This will increase the crop in the third year hugely.

Recently two more types have appeared. 'Frozen' plants (which have been cold-stored) are available between March and June and arrive as bare-root bundles. They should be planted as quickly as possible and kept well watered during their first season. They should fruit within 60 days of being planted.

Misted-tip plants (grown from cuttings) are available in August – see page 117.

Did you know? Most strawberries need short days to form their flower buds and they use a pigment called phytochrome to tell them whether it's day or night.
??Varieties fall into two categories. Most are short-day varieties and crop in June and July. Perpetual varieties ('everbearers') crop in flushes throughout the summer, but these do not have the traditional sweet strawberry flavour. Instead they have the aromatic tang of alpine strawberries. Perpetual-fruiting varieties are normally grown for 2 years only and they don't usually produce runners.

SECRETS OF SUCCESS

- The earlier in the year you plant strawberries, the better the crop in the following year.
- Plant strawberries in rectangular blocks rather than rows — that way they are easier to net.
- Newly planted strawberries are often overrun by ants, so keep an eye on your plants. A drenching of water usually helps.
- Cut down the foliage of perpetual ('everbearing') varieties in early autumn after fruiting has tailed off. Put the foliage in the bin.

VARIETIES OF PERPETUAL STRAWBERRY ('EVERBEARERS')

'Mara des Bois'
Dark-red, medium-sized berries with an alpine strawberry flavour. Crops well and resists mildew.

'Flamenco'
Heavy-yielding, new strawberry with large, firm, sweet fruit that keeps well on the plant. Resistant to verticillium wilt and powdery mildew.

'Finesse'
An even newer variety with heart-shaped berries on long trusses that stand proud of the lush, dense foliage. They ripen evenly and are also easy to pick. Crops from late June through to late August without producing many runners.

For further varieties of strawberry, see February, page 25.

2 Feed Blackcurrants, Pears and Plums with Nitrogen

(early March)

NITROGEN produces leafy growth rather than fruit, so generally it is applied to fruit trees and bushes only if they are greedy feeders. Blackcurrants, pears and plums need a boost in early spring and the easiest way to apply nitrogen with certainty is to use hoof and horn or a general fertilizer. Apply 100g per square metre (3oz per square yard).

These nitrogen-hungry plants all like spring and summer rainfall. If the spring is dry, water them carefully in clement weather by gently tipping a bucket or two of water on the roots a couple of times a week. Always try to keep the water away from the trunk or woody stems – don't splash a hose on them. Do bear in mind that March nights are cool, so any watering should be over and done with by midday.

Did you know? The blackcurrant was first recorded in 1611, growing at Hatfield House in Hertfordshire. The gardener, John Tradescant the Elder, ordered twelve plants from Holland for the Earl of Salisbury's garden. The fruit was generally disliked by most people, however, and did not become popular until the late nineteenth century. The arrival in 1936 of the vitamin C drink Ribena led to mass cultivation, mainly in Herefordshire. Today 30 per cent of the UK's blackcurrants are grown in Herefordshire and most find their way into blackcurrant cordial.

SECRETS OF SUCCESS WITH BLACKCURRANTS

- Blackcurrants are shallow-rooted and struggle in droughts. They prefer cool conditions and rich, heavy soil that holds the moisture. They also enjoy full sun — although they will tolerate light shade.
- Plant 1.5m (5ft) apart. After planting always cut back all the shoots to about 2.5cm (1in) from the ground.
- Water blackcurrants during dry periods in the growing season.
- Feed with nitrogen in spring.
- Hand-weed and mulch around the plants to keep the weeds down and moisture in. Blackcurrants resent competition.
- Prune in late summer — see page 116.

VARIETIES OF BLACKCURRANT

'Ben Connan' ('Ben Sarek' x 'Ben Lomond')
High yields of exceptionally large fruits on a compact bush. Resistant to mildew and leaf-curling midge. Pick mid-July.

'Ben Lomond'
Flowers and fruits late, so will miss the frosts. A heavy crop of large, sweet berries on a compact bush. Mildew-resistant. Pick in late July.

'Ben Sarek'
Compact choice for the smaller garden. Frost- and mildew-resistant, so a good choice for colder sites. Heavy crops of large fruits ready for picking in mid-July.

'Wellington XXX'
This 1913 variety is a vigorous, spreading bush, producing a bumper crop of thick-skinned, sweet, juicy berries, even in hot summers. Pick in mid-July.

3 Prune Redcurrants and Whitecurrants
(mid-March)

REDCURRANTS and whitecurrants are related to the blackcurrant (*Ribes nigrum*) but are derived from two different species, *R. rubrum* and *R. spicatum*. They fruit in a different way, on one-year-old wood and on spurs from older wood, so a permanent framework needs to be preserved. They do not need a procession of young wood like the blackcurrant, so shoots are not cut out at the base.

The objective of pruning redcurrants and whitecurrants is to create a goblet-shaped bush with between eight and ten main branches growing from a stem about 15cm (6in) off the ground. It is traditional to prune them as the sap rises, just as the buds begin to swell. Also, any buds that have been pecked and damaged by birds can be identified once the swelling starts.

Established bushes should have their leaders tipped by removing the top 5–7.5cm (2–3in) to stimulate new growth. All the laterals (side shoots) are then pruned back to one bud and any low branches are cut away at the source. This is the exactly the same method as used for gooseberries (see page 7).

Redcurrants and whitecurrants can suffer from die-back (a

fungal disease). If the wood looks brown and dead when you cut into it, make a cut lower down where the wood is fresh and white. Remove it at source if you need to. If successive cuts reveal that die-back has entered the main stem, sadly the whole bush will need to be removed.

Did you know? The word 'currant' derives from the Greek city of Corinth and describes a small dried grape. Currants were even called 'corinths' in some early English books. The botanist John Parkinson, writing in 1629, is at pains to explain the difference between the dried currant and the fresh currant before extolling their virtues.

SECRETS OF SUCCESS WITH CURRANTS

- Redcurrant bushes thrive in open, sunny positions. However, they are tolerant of shade and they will fruit to a lesser degree on a north-facing wall — although later in the year.
- Plant bushes 1.5m (5ft) apart. They are more tolerant of drier soils than blackcurrants, so lighter dressings of manure (up to 5cm/2in) are best.
- Avoid frost pockets and exposed windy sites, although redcurrant and whitecurrant flowers seem to survive frost.
- Redcurrants crop very heavily, even on poor soil, and one mature bush usually produces plenty — up to 4.5kg (10lb) of fruit. Tie the branches to canes set around each plant to prevent the branches flopping to the ground under the weight of the fruit.
- Net the bushes tightly against bullfinches, blackbirds and thrushes before the fruit starts to ripen.

Organic Tip ✔

Red-, white- and blackcurrants are insect-pollinated. They can self-pollinate but crops are better when insects do the job. Currants (and gooseberries) flower early — beginning in March — at a time when not many flying insects are around. The main agents of pollination then are bumblebees and mining bees. These are quite large insects, so if you haven't lifted the side netting of your fruit cage to allow them access, make sure that the netting has a mesh large enough to allow them through. You will help our endangered bees as well as improving your crop.

VARIETIES

'Jonkheer van Tets' AGM
One of the earliest, bearing heavy crops of large red berries with an excellent flavour. Ripe in July.

'Red Lake'
A mid-season redcurrant producing large, heavy yields of long trusses of juicy berries that are easy to pick. Pick in late July.

'Redstart'
This late-season redcurrant produces heavy yields on an upright bush. It has excellent disease-resistance and its late-flowering habit avoids any frost damage. A slow-growing variety that makes a good choice for smaller gardens. Pick in August.

'Versailles Blanche' (syn. 'White Versailles')
Reliable yields of large, yellow-white berries. Good crops year after year. Pick in early July.

4 Plant an Apricot Tree
(late March)

SPRINGS are coming earlier and earlier, so gardeners should be taking advantage of the situation. This, combined with recent breeding (see Organic Tip, page 45) is making it possible to grow apricots outside in the open rather than up against a warm wall. Commercial orchards planted 15 years ago are now cropping well and making a profit. Now that the ground is beginning to warm up it is the perfect moment to order one of these hardier apricots and to prepare the ground for planting.

The new varieties succeed in well-drained, open ground on good soil. A 5-year-old tree could produce 500 fruits in a sheltered position.

Apricots are self-fertile, so you will need only one tree, but you will have to discipline yourself to hand-pollinate the flowers, because generally apricot blossom arrives early, often before the bees are about to do it for you. It is traditional to use a rabbit's tail for hand-pollination, but a fluffy paintbrush is equally effective. Gently brush each flower when it is fully open (when the pollen is ripe). You won't see it, but pollen is transferred from flower to flower. Be methodical, moving along each branch, and dream of sun-warmed apricots while you do it. A home-grown apricot is utterly different from a bought one. Hand-pollinate on warm, sunny days.

Apricots don't suffer from as many diseases as peaches; bacterial canker and silver leaf are not serious threats. They can be pruned in late winter or early spring if you wish.

Organic Tip ✔

Apricots flower in February and growing them went into a decline in Britain largely due to colder winters. In recent years, however, North American- and Canadian-bred varieties (often with the suffix 'cot') have arrived. These trees can fruit in Britain without a warm wall and commercial production of apricots is the proof. Sainsbury's snapped up the first Kent-grown crop harvested in 2005. Grow one of these modern varieties.

VARIETIES

'Tomcot'
Produces a very heavy crop of large, crimson-flushed fruits which are ripe for picking from around the middle of July. Can be grafted on to Torinel rootstock, which is the latest rootstock for growing apricots. Approximate tree height when mature: 3m (10ft). (See also page 76.)

'Doucouer'
A French variety introduced in 2004, with a good flavour. Height at maturity: 3m (10ft).

'Goldcot'
Recommended for cooler, wetter climates. Hardy, vigorous and resistant to leaf spot, producing good crops of medium–large, golden-yellow, freestone fruit (the stone is not attached to the flesh – a great convenience in the kitchen) in August which will keep in the fridge for several weeks. Height at maturity: 3m (10ft).

Did you know? The apricot almost certainly originated from China, where it still grows wild in the mountains close to Peking. It spread along the Silk Road from east to west and Alexander the Great was said to have brought the fruit from Asia to Greece. From there it travelled to Italy, where Pliny wrote about in I BC. It was also grown and dried in Ancient Egypt. In Britain it became a gentleman's fruit in the late seventeenth century. 'Moorpark' (named after Lord Anson's garden near Watford in Hertfordshire, but often listed as 'Temple') was available by 1777 and continued to be the most widely grown variety for 200 years. Jane Austen even mentioned this fruit in *Mansfield Park*. A warm wall was required and Aynho, a village on the Northamptonshire/Oxfordshire border, boasted a particularly large number of trees on south-facing cottages. The original trees were brought there from Italy by the local squire, Sir Thomas Cartwright (1795–1850), and some still exist today.

SECRETS OF SUCCESS

- Prepare the soil well and incorporate lots of organic matter. Stake and secure with a tree tie as you plant, angling it at 45 degrees to avoid damaging the roots. See page 5.
- Water well in the first growing season.
- Summer warmth is essential for apricots, so find a warm, sheltered position.
- Be prepared to cover your tree when it's in flower if frost is forecast. A fleece blanket is ideal.
- Fruit forms on short spurs that are 2–3 years old, so give your tree at least 4–5 years to produce lots of fruiting wood.
- Thin clusters of apricots down to doubles.

5 Plant a Cherry Tree
(late March)

CHERRIES deserve a wider audience. New breeding and better rootstocks have arrived over the last 40 years or so and this is an excellent time to plant one or more of these recent varieties. Many are now grown on Gisela rootstock, which produces a 3–4m (8–10ft) tree that will fruit after only 3 or 4 years.

Plant cherries in a sunny site on average, well-drained soil. The shallow rootstocks used for all cherries mean that they do not survive in waterlogged ground: they pick up soil-borne root diseases like phytophthora. They also need permanent staking – again due to those shallow roots.

Canadian and British breeders have produced more cold-tolerant varieties that will crop in cooler temperatures, providing white blossom, fruit and autumn colour. They are mostly self-fertile too, so one tree will crop on its own. This makes them an ideal tree for a small garden.

There are two types of cherry. Sweet cherries (*Prunus avium*) need full sun and are generally eaten raw when ripe. Acid cherries (*P. cerasus*) are darker in colour and are normally cooked. They can be grown in shade against a wall. Both types will need a sheltered, warm site. This will attract the bees and, hopefully, protect that early-spring blossom from frost. Acid cherries crop all along the length of one-year-old wood. Sweet cherries crop at the base of one-year-old wood and on older wood.

Did you know? The Japanese revere cherry blossom and hold special ceremonies every spring during a national holiday calculated to coincide with the blossom. The cherry orchards of eighteenth-century England were also popular with tourists. Paddle-steamers would ferry visitors up the River Tamar from Plymouth to see the orchards on the slopes of the valley when the blossom was in its full glory. St Mellion, on the Cornish side of the Tamar, still holds an annual cherry feast every July. One famous cherry, 'Waterloo', was raised by Thomas Andrew Knight of Downton Castle in Herefordshire, the producer of the Downton Strawberry (see page 23). This fine dessert cherry fruited within weeks of the battle in 1815 and is still available – just.

VARIETIES

'Stella' AGM
An older, self-fertile variety with dark-red to black fruit. Early and prolific, it makes a good pollinator for other cherries. Pick in late July. Pollination Group D.

'Sunburst'
A new Canadian-bred, self-fertile dessert variety that produces almost black cherries. These are very large and full of flavour. Not as heavy-cropping as 'Stella'. Pick in July. Group D.

'Summer Sun' AGM
A very hardy variety raised in Norfolk and suited to cold areas. Produces a heavy crop of dark-red fruit with an excellent flavour on a naturally bushy tree. Pick in late summer. Self-fertile. Pollination Group D.

'Celeste'
Perhaps the best variety for a small garden because this compact, almost-dwarf, self-fertile cherry can be pot-grown. It was raised in Canada in 1990 and the dark-red fruits are very good to eat. Ripens early. Pollination Group B/C

Organic Tip ✔

Cherries enjoy radiated heat and light coming up from the ground or off a wall. Place a light-reflective covering on the ground straight after flowering — use white stones or a man-made covering. The reflected light will help pollen-tube growth.

SECRETS OF SUCCESS

- Plant trees or bushes in a sunny site on average—rich, well-drained soil. If your soil is thin, improve it before planting by adding organic matter.
- Protect cherry flowers from frost by covering your trees on cool nights with a double layer of horticultural fleece supported on tall canes, keeping the fleece well above the blossom. This should allow pollinators access to the flowers during the day. Remove the fleece once the blossom has been pollinated and the petals drop.
- Give your tree a very light, sympathetic pruning after harvest — see page 110.
- Keep cherries well watered in the early stages of fruit development; otherwise all the young fruit may fall off in May. Cherries are self-thinning, so leave them to it.
- Feed in mid-spring with a top-dressing of general-purpose fertilizer.
- Few fruits attract as much attention from the birds as cherries do, so you must net. It's easier to net a cherry growing against a wall, if you have one.

6 Plant Raspberries and Other Cane Fruit

(late March)

NOW IS the best time to plant new raspberry canes, but do avoid those anonymous plastic bundles you can buy in garden centres; they may have been sitting there for months in airless, dark, damp conditions. Make sure that you buy certified stock from a good nursery and plant in clement conditions, avoiding frozen or water-logged soil.

Dig in 10cm (4in) of organic matter 30cm (12in) either side of the intended row and erect strong supports at the end. Then make shallow holes and space each cane 35–45cm (14–18in) apart. Spread the roots out and cover with 7.5cm (3in) of soil. Rows need to be at least 1.5–1.8m (5–6ft) apart to allow access. Once planted, always cut each cane back to 22cm (9in) in height to avoid wind rock. On heavy soil, canes can be planted on a raised ridge to improve drainage.

Other cane fruit can also be planted now, including loganberries and tayberries. Both are raspberry × blackberry hybrids. The loganberry is a large, prickly plant that occupies 3.5–4.5m (12–15ft) of space and the long raspberry-like fruit ripens between August and September. It has a sharp flavour and is best cooked or jammed. The larger, sweeter and more aromatic tayberry crops first and the fruit is good for pies, jam or eating fresh.

The tayberry was developed at the Scottish Crops Research Institute, Invergowrie, Scotland, by Derek Jennings and David Mason in the 1970s. It has never become a commercial success because the berries are difficult both to pick by hand and to machine-harvest. If you have room, it's worth planting one. The 'Buckingham Tayberry' is a new thornless variety with smooth canes.

Did you know? The original cross between a blackberry and a raspberry was made accidentally by James Harvey Logan of Santa Cruz, California, in 1881–83. Logan was trying to produce a better blackberry and, while attempting to cross two varieties, he planted both next to a raspberry, thought to be 'Red Antwerp'. The two blackberries, 'Texas Early' and 'Aughinburgh', produced fifty seedlings between them and one, with long red fruit, was named the loganberry. Logan's original hybrid was introduced to Europe in 1897. It proved to be productive but its sharp flavour was not universally popular.

Organic Tip ✔

Always remember that raspberries grow best in slightly acid soil that is well drained and moisture-retentive. The best way to create ideal soil is through the liberal use of bulky organic manure, which is itself acidic and improves both drainage and moisture-retention. Even more organic matter than usual should be added to dry or limy soils.

SECRETS OF SUCCESS

- Choose an open site to attract pollinators: this ensures a heavier crop. Good light will also encourage much sturdier, stronger canes.
- Avoid windy sites. The fruit bruises easily.
- Try to run the rows north–south to minimize shading.
- Clear the site of perennial weeds before planting and improve the fertility of the planting trench with organic matter.
- Plant canes in clement conditions, avoiding frozen or waterlogged soil.
- Cut back newly planted canes to 22cm (9in) to avoid wind rock.
- For summer-fruiting varieties, add sturdy upright supports at the ends of rows and spread wire between them (autumn-fruiting varieties are self-supporting).
- Once established, chop out any canes that wander — especially those that invade the space between the rows.
- If new canes come up with mottled foliage, dig them up: it is almost certainly caused by a virus.
- For advice on cutting back autumn-fruiting and thinning summer-fruiting raspberries, see pages 21 and 114.
- Raspberries come from northern Europe and they prefer cooler summers — which is why they often do well in Scotland. Mulching helps to keep the soil cool and moist. Partially rotted grass clippings make a suitable mulch.
- Pick your fruit on a dry day.

VARIETIES OF SUMMER-FRUITING RASPBERRIES

'Tulameen'
Conveniently follows on from the strawberries, producing large, tasty fruit. Crops well.

'Glen Ample' AGM
This mid-season variety produces heavy crops of very large fruit on strong, spine-free, upright canes.

'Glen Rosa'
A new mid-season, spine-free variety, producing an abundance of bright, high-quality, medium-sized fruit. Very disease-resistant, so ideal for organic production.

'Malling Admiral'
The popular favourite, due to its excellent flavour and dark-red fruit. Quite a tall cane, although completely spine-free. Probably the best choice if you are restricted to one summer variety.

For varieties of autumn-fruiting raspberry, see February, page 21.

APRIL

*T*he earlier-flowering tree fruits (such as plums and pears) begin to show blossom now, but April can be a cruel month and there are often frosts that ruin the blossom, resulting in either a poor crop or no crop at all. A single tree could be fleeced, but when there are several it's best to opt for later-flowering varieties.

There are differences in temperature within every plot. Cold air always falls to the lowest point and this is why so many orchards are on south- or west-facing slopes: the trees not only like the extra drainage but also avoid spring frosts. Orchard fruits are never planted into the dip at the foot of a slope, which is where cold air collects.

So all fruit should be planted in the most frost-free place in your garden, but light levels also have to be good. Nectar flows in sunshine, attracting bees to pollinate your trees.

1 Fleece Strawberries
(early April)

IF APRIL is warm and sunny, early varieties of strawberries will begin to flower and this puts them in the danger zone. If the flowers get frosted they turn into black-eyed Susans (so they are very obvious) and they never bear fruit. Your crop is lost. Frosts are commonplace in April – they can even strike as late as the second half of May – so strawberries always need protection. Pay special heed to the weather forecast and prepare to roll out the fleece as needed. Horticultural fleece, one of the very best modern inventions, is inexpensive, light, and it does its job well.

You may also like to continue the war on slugs by watering on slug nematodes (tiny parasitic worms) around your strawberries. If so, wait until late April when the soil and air temperatures are warmer. Research has shown that a warm, damp day is best and the optimum time is 4pm, when the April sun is cooling off. You won't see lots of dead slugs, as everything happens underground, but the effects last for 6 weeks or so and, when the slugs are gone from the plot, the nematodes also die.

Did you know? Looks are not everything when it comes to strawberries. The best-looking strawberries are produced by the Indian strawberry, *Duchesnea indica*. Named for Antoine Duchesne, a Frenchman who somehow managed to write a monograph on strawberries in the middle of the French Revolution (see also page 23), its fruit are perfectly shaped, perfectly red and utterly tasteless.

SECRETS OF SUCCESS

• For advice on planting and caring for strawberries, see also February, page 23; March, page 36; May, page 72; June, page 93; and August, page 117.

VARIETIES

For varieties of strawberry, see February, page 25, and March, page 38.

2 Avoid Spraying
(early April)

APRIL IS a key month for the birds in our gardens because most begin to nest now. Chaffinches, blue tits, coal tits, wrens, robins and blackbirds will have their broods to feed this month. All baby birds (even those of seed-eating birds) need a diet of invertebrates until they fledge. They are in the nest for roughly

21 days, during which time an average brood of seven blue tits will consume 10,000 insects and grubs – and there may be several nests in and near your garden. Gooseberries, fruit trees, currants, raspberries and strawberries will be frisked daily. When a bird finds a good source of food (young sawfly grubs on a gooseberry, for instance), she or he will ferry back and forth between there and the nest, cleaning up the whole colony.

This is far more effective pest control than spraying because you inevitably miss some. In time, insects also develop chemical resistance, so the spray becomes next to useless. Worse still, the balance of your garden is completely ruined. It relies upon a complex set of relationships between predator and pest – the ladybird needs the aphid, for instance.

Sprays exterminate both pest and predator – and this also happens if you use organic or 'green' soft soap, mustard and garlic sprays. However, the pest can bounce back quickly – in a few days – because most have short life cycles. Aphids, for example, can produce forty generations in a growing season, given the correct conditions. Predators' life cycles are much longer and most produce only one or two generations per year, so they take far longer to recover. With no predators, the pests get the upper hand and you get more problems, not fewer.

Relying on Mother Nature is the best option for the home gardener. This is what generations of gardeners did in the past – and it works!

Did you know? Red-breasted robins are very aggressive birds and will fight to the death over their territories. This is why they sing so persistently — to deter any incomers. Their most prized possession is the spindle tree (*Euonymus europaeus*) because the bright pink-and-orange fruits are the most nutritious of any hedgerow plant.

CREATING A GOOD ECO-SYSTEM

- Building up a good eco-system relies on how attractive your garden is to insect life, both above and below the ground.
- Make it a chemical-free zone.
- Plant diversely, using trees, shrubs, perennials, evergreens, grasses, ferns, annuals and bulbs to attract a wide range of insects.
- Have undisturbed areas — hedge bottoms, wilder banks and some long grass, for instance — where insects and small animals can hibernate.
- Plant different areas of the garden according to conditions — shade-lovers in a shady spot, moisture-lovers in damp areas, etc.
- The boundaries between differently planted areas are particularly good for insect diversity. Try to add new areas.
- Provide blossom from early in the year until late. Start with snowdrops, crocus and hellebores and end with winter-flowering shrubs like *Lonicera purpusii*.

> ### *Organic Tip* ✔
>
> *About half of all aphid species target a certain plant. The large lupin aphid, for example, rarely goes on to other plants. If you see a colony in your garden and it really troubles you, don't use a spray — green or chemical — and don't try to spray them off with water. Instead, rub them through your fingers. Wear gloves if you are squeamish. Aphids have a fragile feeding tube called a stylet and once this is broken, they die. It is their Achilles heel.*

3 Blossom and Bees
(mid-April)

THE IMPORTANCE of pollination cannot be stressed enough. Without it, you won't get any fruit.

Pollination simply means the transfer of pollen from the stamens, or male parts, of a flower to the pistil, or female part, of a flower. The pollen cannot, though, arrive on any part of the pistil; it must land on a specialized surface designed to receive pollen – the stigma. Once it has arrived, the pollen grows tiny, microscopic pollen tubes into the ovary and fertilizes the ovules – but only if the pollen and ovules are compatible. Compatibility is under genetic control; it works on the same principles as our own immune system.

Some fruit trees, such as nectarines, can be fertilized by their own pollen; they are self-compatible. Some, such as most sweet cherries, are self-incompatible. They must be cross-fertilized by pollen from another variety of the same fruit – it must be another variety and not just another plant of the same variety. This is because all the plants of a single variety are clonal – that is, they have been propagated vegetatively and are genetically identical.

So, pollen that lands on the stigma of another plant of the same variety will be rejected because the stigma recognizes the pollen as itself. Other fruits, such as some apple varieties, show partial incompatibility: they can pollinate themselves at a pinch, but fruit is much better if they are cross-pollinated. These are best treated as fully self-incompatible because we want as much fruit as possible.

We can manage pollination in the fruit garden using a few simple rules.

The first is to know which fruits are self-fertile and which are not. You can have single specimens of self-fertile fruits but you may need to plant two varieties of self-incompatible fruits. For example, all apple varieties are divided into seven pollination groups according to when they flower, Group A being very early and Group G very late. All the varieties in one group flower at about the same time, ensuring that all-important cross-pollination. Flowering also overlaps partly with varieties in some adjacent groups, so a variety in Group C will very probably be pollinated by one in Group B or Group D. Even if varieties flower together, some pairings are not compatible, though. 'Cox's Orange Pippin' will not cross with 'Holstein' or 'Kidd's Orange Red', for example. Some very good apples, like 'Bramley Seedling', are triploid (they have three sets of chromosomes) and produce hardly any viable pollen, so they make ineffective pollen partners. If you wish to grow a 'Bramley', you will need to plant a trio, using two other varieties in order to cross all three. Other bountiful varieties are biennial – they produce a bumper crop every second year – which also means that they flower poorly every other year and they are ineffective pollinators then.

Apples, pears, some plums, blueberries and most cherries need cross-pollination. Cherries, in particular, have a complicated incompatibility system, but new varieties are self-fertile, which helps a lot. Peaches and apricots are self-fertile.

Besides the plants and their flowers, we also need to think about the agents of pollination. The vast majority of pollination in the fruit garden is carried out by insects and particularly by bees. The list of bee-pollinated fruit is almost endless: apples, pears, plums, gages, damsons, cherries, quince, peaches, apricots, strawberries, raspberries, blueberries, blackcurrants and many more. The exceptions are nuts such as hazelnuts and walnuts, which are wind-pollinated. They produce vast quantities of pollen and rely on luck and the four winds to transfer it to the stigma.

Insect-pollinated plants have learned to improve the chances of pollination by providing the pollinator with rewards of energy-rich nectar and protein-rich pollen. Pollen and nectar are positioned in the flower to maximize the chances of transfer when the pollinator visits. The pollinator moves from flower to flower, picking up pollen from stamens and depositing it on stigmas as it goes.

Bees are critically important to the fruit-grower. There are about 250 species in Britain and most of them visit flowers, pollinating as they go. They travel some distance when they forage; honeybees can travel 6km (4 miles) or more away from the hive, but journeys by other bees are much shorter. Solitary bees, such as mining bees and potter bees, may travel no more than 200m (220yd). Bumblebees can travel a little further – perhaps 1km (? mile). So if you have space for only one variety of a self-incompatible fruit, you may be able to rely on pollen from trees in the neighbourhood, but some fruits, such as cherries, are not widely grown, so the chances of bees bringing pollen to your plant are much lower.

Did you know? We look on the honeybee as a model of industry, but bumblebees are far more efficient pollinators. They fly in cooler temperatures, so early-flowering fruit often relies on them rather than on honeybees. When visiting a flower, bumblebees frequently vibrate their wings violently to shake pollen free. This is called 'buzz pollination' because of the sound the bee makes.

Organic Tip ✔

Encourage wild bees into your garden. Springtime blossom is excellent for this, but to get them really visiting you need to provide flowers from early spring, when the pregnant queens emerge from hibernation, until the new young queens go into hibernation in autumn. Nest sites include holes in walls, mossy vegetation in hedge bases and even old mouse nests.

SECRETS OF SUCCESS

- Late-pollination groups are often recommended for frost-prone gardens; however, most popular varieties of apple tend to be in Pollination Group C.
- Use a reputable fruit-grower who knows a lot about varieties — including pollination groups. Size and vigour are restricted by rootstocks (see page 109), but variety also plays a part. Triploid apple trees (like 'Bramley Seedling') make large trees. Pears are fussier about their pollination partners than apples.
- In very built-up areas where there is a lot of top fruit in surrounding gardens, there is usually plenty of pollen. You may get away with planting just one fruit tree — but it's a gamble.

4 Grow Fruit in Containers
(mid-April)

THIS IS an excellent time to buy container-grown fruit trees and bushes. A lot of modern breeding has gone into producing dwarf varieties suitable for small gardens and, if your plot is tiny, these can be extremely worthwhile. The Californian plant-breeder Floyd Zaiger has bred a series of dwarf fruit trees that produce full-size fruit. These rounded trees can be grown in the ground and after 7 years will reach 1.5m (5ft) in height. Grown in pots, they will stay even smaller. Their diminutive size makes them ideal patio plants.

However, if you go down the container route you have to be extra vigilant about plant care. Growing in a container exposes plants to drier, hotter conditions in summer and colder conditions in winter. It is much more stressful for the plant than growing in the ground. Nutrients soon become scarce, so feeding and watering are important.

Most dwarf fruit comes ready containerized. If you want to re-pot it, use wood or terracotta: both are far kinder to the roots in summer and winter. Black plastic pots should not be used: the dark plastic absorbs the heat too efficiently and does not protect against frost. Aim for a pot 38–55cm (15–22in) in diameter.

The big difference between the care of container and open-ground fruit trees is that container fruit must be root-pruned occasionally to maintain fruit production. This is done in late autumn.

These dwarf varieties give every gardener the chance to raise some of their own peaches and nectarines. Pot-grown fruits are easier to protect *in situ* against frost, birds and high winds. Alternatively, you can move them into a cold conservatory or slightly warm greenhouse. Dwarf cherries and smaller fig varieties can also be grown in a pot. Figs should be taken inside in early winter.

South-facing walls are always cited as the best against which to place container-grown fruit, but in hot summers this can frazzle plants. I would advocate a west-facing or south-west-facing wall, but avoid north-facing walls: these are too sunless. Also avoid east-facing walls as they get the sun early and thaw out frosted flowers and buds far too quickly.

Did you know? Potted fruit is nothing new. Grapes were often grown in pots (using methods described by the garden writer John Claudius Loudon in 1835) and when the trusses were ripe, the whole plant was taken into the dining room, pot and all, so that guests could pick their own ripe fruit.

VARIETIES

Dwarf Cherry
'Garden Bing'
Large, dark-red clusters of cherries that are ready to pick in late July. The snow-white blossom appears in April. (Do not confuse with the full-size 'American Bing' varieties.) Self-fertile.

Fig
'Rivers Brown Early'
Large, pear-shaped brown fruit with a purple tinge. A reliable, early, abundant variety rescued from the famous Rivers Nursery near Sawbridgeworth in Hertfordshire when it was demolished for development. Self-fertile.

Nectarine
'Rubis'
Large, lance-shaped and colourful yellow fruit flushed with red. The pink blossom appears in March so, although self-fertile, you will need to hand-pollinate (see page 44).

Peach
'Bonanza'
Genetic dwarf peach, bred in California. It produces a 'mop head' of full-sized leaves, a mass of pink blossom and full-sized fruits. Self-fertile.

SECRETS OF SUCCESS

- Choose a rugged, weatherproof container and make sure that it has drainage holes. Add a layer of crocks at the bottom to assist drainage further and stand your pot on feet – this allows surplus water to escape.
- Use loam-based John Innes No. 3 for your compost. This retains moisture more efficiently than peat-based composts and delivers nutrients more slowly. Firm down well and always leave at least 5cm (2in) at the top to allow for mulching and watering. Add 2.5cm (1in) of well-rotted compost or manure and a little general fertilizer.
- Water regularly from March onwards. Start with a little at first and then increase the amount. Allow a little to run out of the bottom to stop the build-up of harmful salts.
- Feed with a high-potash (tomato) fertilizer fortnightly from April until late August to encourage flower and fruit.
- Also use a foliar seaweed feed every 2 weeks to strengthen and toughen the foliage. This prevents pests and diseases.
- Figs should be taken in during December.
- At leaf fall, remove all remaining figs larger than small peas. Leaving them on will reduce next season's crop and may cause die-back.
- Take out growing tips of all new-season shoots on peaches, nectarines, cherries and figs around the middle to end of June, a little earlier than you would with open-ground trees.

5 Beat the Spring Drought
(late April)

BRITISH weather is unpredictable and we can't do anything about varying or erratic temperatures, or sunlight hours. We just have to accept what we get stoically. However, we can conserve moisture by mulching and spring is often a good time to do this, as we can get a period of drought. Mulching will also keep weed growth down. Late April is ideal, because if a mulch is applied too early it tends to get washed away.

Mulching needs to be well timed: it should follow a period of heavy rain and the soil must be warm. In dry conditions you may need to soak the ground before applying a mulch. Those on lighter soil in the drier eastern half of England will benefit most; those in wetter areas may not need to bother. If you're on alluvial soil close to a river, the ground may already be very moist due to a high water table.

Mulches decompose and as they do so they use up nitrogen in the soil, which may cause plant stress. If well-rotted manure and garden compost are being used the decomposition process should be more or less complete, so there will be plenty of nutrients on offer from the organic matter. However, some mulches (like ornamental bark) deliver very little in the way of nutrition. If using bark or gravel, always add a nitrogen-rich feed before spreading the mulch.

Did you know? Warmth encourages the development of the pollen tube, so warm Mays are what fruit-growers pray for.

Organic Tip ✔

Pears are the most demanding fruit trees when it comes to moisture and they often do well in low-lying river valleys where the soil is rich. They also like warmth. Always water pears from the moment the flower buds burst until 6 weeks after blossoming to improve the yield. Gently tip one bucket of water on the roots of each pear tree every day in dry spells.

SECRETS OF SUCCESS

• Don't mound mulch up right against the trunks of trees and shrubs: it will kill them. Swirl a 5cm (2in) layer around them instead.
• Weed and aerate the soil before applying mulch. If it's a mulch that offers little or nothing (bark, gravel, sawdust, etc.), add a nitrogen-rich fertilizer first.
• The downside of mulching is that it can harbour slugs and snails – so mulching near slug-prone plants is not a good thing.
• Local authorities are producing green waste material from garden refuse collections. This should be worth trying for many, unless you are an organic gardener: it cannot be guaranteed chemical-free.

6 Remove Protective Coverings from Peaches and Nectarines

(late April)

MOST OLDER and heritage varieties of peach, nectarine and almond are prone to a fungal disease called peach leaf curl (*Taphrina deformans*). In early spring the leaves produce red or white blisters and then the whole leaf curls up before dropping to the ground. This devastating disease effectively defoliates the tree and starves it of food. Although a second crop of leaves follows (and they often stay healthy), the damage has already been done and the tree will fail to produce much fruit.

The fungus overwinters on the shoot tips of the plant, especially in the scales surrounding young buds. The fungus is transferred from the bud scales to the young leaves in spring by rain, where it causes the characteristic deformed leaves. The fungus grows, sporulates, and the spores are returned to the shoot surfaces to begin the cycle again. Most experienced fruit-growers opt for prevention. If you can keep the rain off the peach tree in winter the spores are not transferred to the young leaves. Cover the whole tree with glass or polythene over winter to keep the buds dry. Leave the sides open to encourage air flow. The covering also protects the early blossom from frost. Also, gather up and destroy infected leaves early so that the fungus cannot sporulate. See also page 153.

Now is the time to remove your cover and allow the tree to form healthy leaves. Older peach varieties are much more prone to peach leaf curl than newer varieties, and nectarines are more difficult to grow than peaches.

Did you know? Peach leaf curl is caused by just one of a specialized group of fungi. They all disrupt the plants' hormone systems and cause distorted growth. Pocket plums – distorted fruit with a hollow, pocket-like side – are caused by *Taphrina pruni*. Cherries and pears suffer attacks from other specialized *Taphrina* species.

Organic Tip ✔

Do not be tempted to use the traditional fix for peach leaf curl – Bordeaux mixture – even though it is still approved for organic use (though no longer recommended). It is very high in copper, which is toxic to many beneficial creatures, especially frogs and toads.

SECRETS OF SUCCESS

- Wall-trained trees generally crop much more reliably for most and it is worth buying a ready-trained, fan-shaped tree (see page 119).
- Always protect the blossom from frost. Hand-pollinate, because there are few (if any) pollinators about.
- Water regularly once the fruit begins to swell.
- Thin the fruit twice during the growing season – at hazelnut size in about May and then at walnut size in June – so that they are well spaced.
- Prune carefully (see page 110), taking some of the older branches out. Create an airy middle – this will lessen the chance of fungal diseases because the wood will dry out better.
- If leaves do curl, pick them up and bin them. Good husbandry is the best prevention.

VARIETIES OF PEACH RESISTANT TO PEACH LEAF CURL

'Avalon Pride'

A chance seedling found growing wild in woods near Seattle in 1981, this outstanding, breakthrough variety is strongly resistant to leaf curl disease. The large fruit is ready in August. If grown on 'St Julian' rootstock, it is less susceptible to frost damage.

'Red Wing'

This forms a large tree and yields well, producing almost completely dark-red fruit with a superb flavour. Late-flowering, so good for colder sites. Has some leaf curl resistance.

TRADITIONAL VARIETIES OF PEACH

'Peregrine' AGM

Reliable, tried-and-tested variety with delicious, large, white-fleshed fruit ready in late summer. A good garden cultivar.

'Rochester' AGM

The best all-rounder for under cover and outdoors, with firm, yellow flesh and crimson-flushed skin.

MAY

This is the most glorious month in the garden and your fruit will be full of promise. Crops will always be better if May is warm and sunny, but you will have to be vigilant about watering well if this is the case. Watering while fruit is setting is extremely important – drought now will really affect your crops. Don't dribble a hose over your plants or sprinkle them. Try to use sun-warmed water on fruit trees, gently tipping one whole bucket over the roots every 3 days or so. This is far more effective than a cold drenching with mains water at this time of year.

However, May nights can still be cold, so evening watering can cause a chill at the roots. If possible, water in the first half of the day when temperatures are mild. Pears, strawberries and black-currants are thirsty plants, so give them priority. Try to keep water away from the foliage, as splashes could spread fungal diseases.

Watch out for late frosts and be prepared to cover blossom with fleece if necessary.

1 Straw and Net Strawberries
(early May)

GROWING strawberries is very worthwhile, but you won't get a crop unless you protect them from the three main enemies: the rain, the slug and the blackbird.

The best way to protect fruit from rain damage is to cushion them on a bed of straw and this is best applied now on a dry, fine day. Simply lift up the foliage and the forming fruit trusses and lightly arrange the straw underneath. If the bale is very tightly packed, open up the straw with your hands. Try to avoid musty bales. You need about half a bale for one 2.4 × 1.2m (8 × 4ft) bed.

Once the straw is down, netting can be done too. The easiest system relies on a set of short, sturdy stakes (about 60cm/2ft high). Arrange these to form a neat grid with roughly 60cm (2ft) between each stake. Pop a small plant pot over each stake – terracotta ones look far more decorative than plastic. Then place black plastic netting over the pots so that the netting is held above the fruit: this will repel aerial invasion. Thread long bamboo canes along each edge so that these rest on the ground to form a mini fruit cage that you can lift on and off in seconds. The canes will also prevent birds from creeping underneath.

When your protection system is in position, keep an eye on your fruit in case botrytis strikes. If you see any grey fluffy mould on the berries, cut them off and bin them. Check over the rest of the crop.

Strawberry plants form the next year's flower buds after they have finished fruiting for the year, a process that is light-dependent. So, once the crop has finished, remove all the straw. Then cut away all the leaves close to the crowns, being careful not to damage them, and feed with a potash-rich fertilizer such as comfrey tea (see page 163). Your plants will have fresh foliage within 10 days. Cutting back also helps to clean the bed of aphids and this will help to prevent virus.

For advice on dealing with slugs, see page 55.

Did you know? The name 'strawberry' is derived not from straw but from an Old English word meaning 'to stray', because of their habit of producing runners and straying off.

Organic Tip ✔

If you are going to water strawberries, always do so in the first part of the day because slugs become active at dusk and like to glide over wet surfaces. Watering in the evening encourages trouble.

SECRETS OF SUCCESS

- Be vigilant in watching out for mould. Remove any affected fruit as soon as you see it.
- Pick ripe fruit regularly — aim for every other day.
- Always remove any strawberry plants with mottled, ringed or yellow-veined foliage — these are symptoms of virus.

VARIETIES

For varieties of strawberry, see February, page 25, and March, page 38.

2 Tend Pears and All Wall-trained Fruit

(mid-May)

WALL-TRAINED fruit is usually positioned against sunny walls and it is always going to be short of water in May, even when the weather is wet, because walls shelter the ground from the rain and then act like a wick in dry spells, drawing water from the soil. Try to get into a regime of regular watering, especially with young trees, which will not have developed deep roots. Trees that are decades old may have a root system that's capable of accessing water held deeper in the ground.

It's well worth making the effort to water well, for if trees become drought-stressed they shed their fruit early. If you can nurse them through May and June far less will drop off. Pears in particular really love moisture, so water them from the moment the flower buds burst until 6 weeks after blossoming to improve the yield. Gently tip one bucket of water on each pear tree every day in dry spells.

Most trees shed fruit in June as a natural process – it's known as the June drop. However, if the fruit set is very heavy it is worth thinning at the end of June–early July; see page 84. Plums can be so laden that the branches snap and many old trees are propped up on wooden supports; this could be an option with trees in open ground.

The most common shape for wall-training is the fan, which radiates from the base of the tree. This must be kept in shape and any growth that is straying away from the wall should be nipped back now. Either rub it off with your fingers or snip it, sterilizing the secateurs after every tree.

Dipping them in boiling water is my system, but some people use bleach. Keep the growth tight against the wall throughout summer.

For advice on pruning and shaping wall-trained fruit, see page 119.

Did you know?   Training exotic fruit trees (like pomegranates, oranges, peaches and figs) began in France, but by the seventeenth century it had become widely practised in the Netherlands. Most of the early fruit trees grown by British pioneers like John Tradescant the Elder were imported from Holland. When William of Orange was crowned King of England in 1689 the two countries forged much closer links and soon fruit-training became popular in England too. Many walled gardens had their walls raised and buttressed to accommodate wall-trained fruit.

SECRETS OF SUCCESS WITH WALL-TRAINED FRUIT

- Buy top-quality fan-trained or cordon-trained trees from a reputable fruit specialist. Try to go and choose your tree personally. They are expensive, but buying one of these will save you years when compared with buying and training small one-year-old trees (or 'maidens', as they are known).
- Add supports before or when planting.
- Spend time keeping your trees in shape – see page 119.
- Water your trees throughout the growing season for the first few years of their life.
- If disease strikes, tidy up any diseased material thoroughly.
- Be prepared to thin your fruit.

FAN-TRAINED VARIETIES FOR A WARM WALL

Apricot
'Flavorcot'
Specially bred for the cooler UK climate. Large, egg-sized, orange-red fruits with excellent flavour. Late-flowering and frost-resistant, so you should always get a crop. Harvest in August. Look for trees grafted on to Mont Clare rootstock.

Apricot
'Tomcot'
An early-cropping apricot giving a very heavy crop of large, crimson-flushed fruits which are ripe for picking from around the middle of July. Look for trees grafted on to Mont Clare, a dwarfing rootstock, as these are suitable for training. (Torinel rootstock is best for full-sized trees – see page 45.)

Cherry
'Sunburst'
This very dark cherry has almost black fruit with a rich flavour. Net against birds in May and harvest in early July. Self-fertile. Pollination Group D.

Nectarine
'Snowqueen'
This new French variety crops heavily. It ripens in late July and is considered to have the best nectarine flavour. Protect from winter rainfall to control leaf curl. Can also be grown under glass. Look for trees grafted on to Mont Clare rootstock.

3 Plant Blueberries
(mid-May)

BLUEBERRIES have acquired super-food status in recent years because they are packed with antioxidants. They produce a useful crop over

4–6 weeks in late July and August (following on from strawberries), when soft fruit is generally in short supply. Choose your water-on plant food wisely. Some nitrogen-rich feeds only promote leafy growth. These are ideal for boosting young yew hedges, cabbages and container-grown topiary, but for flowers and fruit you need to use a potash-rich liquid tomato food.

It is quite possible to grow them, but there is one major drawback. Blueberries are members of the heather family (*Ericaceae*) that grow wild in the heaths and forests of temperate North America, which means that they enjoy a cool, moist root run in well-drained, humus-rich, acid (pH 4.5–5.5) soil. You have to give them these conditions in order to grow them successfully in the garden, which means growing them in containers for most of us.

Wooden containers tend to be better for blueberries than terracotta ones: the latter get warm and absorb heat. Place a plastic sheet in the bottom of the planter and run it some 10cm (4in) up the sides. Cut a few holes in the base to ensure slow but steady drainage. Add ericaceous compost, plant and then mulch well with leaf mould, if you can, to help keep the root run cool and moist. Water with rainwater only.

Blueberries are long-lived plants. They fruit on branches and side shoots that were produced in the previous year. Prune in winter when the plant is dormant, removing the old, tired woody growth that has fruited for 2 years or more and any other weak or damaged stems. Take out any branches that are crossing or congested in the centre of the bush. Young bushes are not normally pruned for the first 3 years.

The varieties on offer (bred from *Vaccinium corymbosum* – the northern highbush blueberry) are subdivided into early-, mid- and late-season kinds and, although blueberries are partly self-fertile, you get a better crop when cross-pollination takes place. Ideally you want two varieties from the same group, and mid-season and late varieties are the most useful. Mine are usually pollinated by a small rusty-backed bee, *Bombus pascuorum* (the Brown-banded Carder Bee), so it's important that they are placed in sunlight to encourage the nectar.

Did you know? Blueberries are recent arrivals in Britain. The first plants were donated by Canada in 1951 to help economic recovery following the Second World War. They came from Lulu Island, just south of Vancouver, and were accepted by the Trehane Nursery, based on acid heathland at Wimborne in Dorset, which went on to become the first to grow blueberries commercially in Britain. They began selling them in 1957. Amazingly, some of the original bushes still survive.

SECRETS OF SUCCESS

- Blueberries do not require heavy feeding. In April, lightly sprinkle a granular fertilizer suitable for acid-loving plants (e.g. Vitax conifer and shrub fertilizer) over the soil surface. Alternatively, a liquid feed (e.g. Miracid) will do just as well.
- If you garden organically, avoid any fertilizers that might contain lime, such as manure, chicken manure and blood, fish and bone. Use hoof and horn instead.
- Water bushes well, but don't allow them to become waterlogged. Use at least 4.5 litres (1 gallon) of rainwater per container every week in summer. Tapwater is too alkaline for blueberries.
- Protect them from excessive winter wet by moving them close to a wall. They are very hardy, but they resent having cold, wet roots.
- Marauding blackbirds love to strip the fruit. Net your plants or put them in a fruit cage.

VARIETIES

'Bluecrop'
The most widely grown variety. Tall, producing a heavy crop of large, light-blue berries with a good flavour. Mid-season.

'Chandler'
A bushy variety that produces much larger fruit – about twice the size of most blueberries. Mid–late-season.

'Patriot'
A rugged variety recommended for heavier, wetter soils and colder areas. Produces large, slightly flat, velvety berries with firm flesh and an excellent flavour. Mid-season fruit, but can flower early.

'Herbert'
Heavy, compact clusters of very large, dark-blue, highly flavoured fruit on a low bush with a spreading habit. Mid-season. Superb autumn colour.

4 Try Some Melons
(mid-May)

MELONS are a challenge for any gardener and success can never be assured. However, if you are a keen fruit-grower with a cold frame in a sunny position or a greenhouse, this is the time to think about acquiring some plants or sowing some seeds.

There are three types of melon. Honeydew varieties have firm yellow flesh. Musk melons have yellow- or green-netted skin and they are the most difficult to grow, even under glass. Cantaloupe melons, which have rough skin and orange-tinted flesh, are the easiest group to grow.

Warmth and water are the keys. All members of the cucurbit family will photosynthesize only in warm temperatures, so it's vital to boost the warmth early in their lives.

Melon plants can normally be acquired in May, but sowing your own now will also work, even though it is a little late (April is best). Melon seed germination is good, so put one seed, pointed end down, in a 7.5cm (3in) watered pot of airy seed-sowing compost and cover with a thin layer of vermiculite. When the plant has three or four true leaves, plant in a cold frame or greenhouse, spacing them 90cm (3ft) apart. If planting in a frame, harden them off by putting them somewhere sheltered during the day for at least a week before planting.

Melons have to be trained and pruned so that they bear good-quality fruit and stay within their allotted space. Pinch out the growing tip at the fifth leaf. As side shoots form, pinch out all but the strongest four and train them to occupy the desired space. Pinch out again; secondary shoots, on which the flowers form, will then grow; pinch the secondary shoots out two leaves beyond the developing fruit.

Organic Tip ✔

You can open the greenhouse or cold frame during the day when the melons are in flower to allow pollinating insects to visit. The drier air helps pollination too.

Did you know? Melons produce male and female flowers. The male flowers (held on longer stems) are produced first and then female flowers (each with a small, bulbous baby swelling at the base) follow. Pollen has to move from the male to the female: the cluster of stamens in a male flower is large enough to break off and hold between your finger and thumb — just dab it on to the stigma of the female flowers.

SECRETS OF SUCCESS

- Choose a reliable Cantaloupe variety.
- Give melons a warm position that gets lots of sun. However, greenhouse melons benefit from being shaded, as the intense heat under glass can scorch them.
- Water your melons often and feed them with a tomato fertilizer every 2 weeks to encourage strong growth and more flowers.
- Plant in a raised bed — these warm up faster. Or use a growbag, two plants per bag. Bring your bags inside for 3 weeks before planting up so that the contents warm up.
- Train the plants vertically, and once the fruit is grapefruit-sized, use onion netting (or something similar) to support it.
- Fruit quality suffers if you try to ripen too many fruits on each plant, so restrict the number of fruit. Cold-frame melons should bear only four fruits. Greenhouse melons can produce six.
- Melons develop an aroma when they are ripe, so use your nose to decide when to harvest them. They also get a woody stem that starts to split.

5 Install a Codling Moth Trap
(late May)

MANY OF you will have bitten into an apple and found an annoying little dark-headed white caterpillar in the middle – or worse still, half a white caterpillar. These are the maggot-like grubs of the inconspicuous grey and brown Codling moth (*Cydia pomonella*). The adult Codling moths – which measure about 1cm (?in) – emerge in late May and early June and lay their eggs on or near developing fruits between June and mid-July. They fly and mate on warm, still evenings when the temperature is above 13°C (55°F). When evening temperatures reach 15.5°C (60°F), conditions are the most conducive to egg-laying. Eggs are laid singly on leaf or fruit surfaces; then the caterpillars hatch out and eat into the fruit. Once they have had their fill, they overwinter in leaf litter or under loose flakes of bark and they pupate the following spring. Codling moths can also attack quince and walnut, but these are rarely infested to any great extent.

In order to thwart these pests, commercial growers hang up Codling moth traps, which alert them to the presence of the moths and capture some of them. The size of a commercial orchard means that when numbers build up the growers still have to spray with insecticide, but they need less because the traps have disrupted the breeding cycle. The home gardener, however, with only a couple of apple or pear trees, may solve the problem entirely by just using a trap. The open-sided boxes are available from garden suppliers and need to be hung in the tree in May. Each one contains a pellet that emits female pheromones at a constant rate, attracting male moths into the trap. The sticky sheet on the bottom traps the male when he homes in on the pellet, hopefully before he has found a female to breed with.

Did you know? Codling moths are the most serious problem in apple production throughout the world. In parts of America (such as Utah) the moths produce five generations per year. In Britain we can get two generations, but only if the first is early enough to be at the cocoon stage by the beginning of July.

SECRETS OF SUCCESS

- Five traps are recommended for a 5-acre orchard and the advice is to hang one at the edge with the rest in the middle. One trap should be enough for most gardens, however.
- Hang your traps in the upper third of the tree.
- Check your traps every day until you find the first moth and then you will know they are on the wing.
- Traps can be stored in early August and refills (sticky sheets and pheromone pellets) can be bought for subsequent years.

6 Thin Fruit
(from late May)

WHEN WE look at a tree laden with fruit, a pleasant glow comes over us. However, we should not let quantity overwhelm us: quality is much more desirable. We do not want the tree or bush to become so exhausted that it rests for 2 or 3 years. With this in mind, it's best to thin out your fruit so that the tree or bush produces a top-grade crop. Depending on the type of fruit, thinning should take place from late May, throughout June.

Gooseberries often yield a bumper crop of small fruits. Pick every other one towards the end of May and cook them, then leave the rest to grow larger. If you're planning to allow your gooseberries to colour up and become really ripe, net the bush after thinning.

Nectarines, plums, peaches, damsons and gages should be thinned twice – once when the fruit is the size of a hazelnut and then again in late May when the fruit is about 2.5cm (1in) in length or golf-ball size. Try to create a 5–7.5cm (2–3in) gap between individual fruits by snipping some of them away with scissors. Do not pull them off: you may destroy next year's fruit buds. Peaches growing along the same branch should be 22cm (9in) apart.

With apples, the number may depend on the tree. Many old apple trees with triploid blood (like the magnificent 'Bramley Seedling') bear a heavy crop every other year. These trees are probably best left to their own devices. All apples and pears will shed fruit in June in a natural thinning process (the June drop) and for this reason apple- and pear-thinning is best left until mid-June. Some varieties shed their fruit later and thinning can take place right up to mid-July and still be effective. Final thinnings of dessert apples should leave 10–15cm (4–6in) between fruit. Large cooking apples often need to be spaced to 15–22cm (6–9in).

Pears need less thinning than apples and the time to start is after the June drop. However, you must wait for pears to turn downwards before thinning them, so that you can be sure that the fruit has set. Usually pears are thinned to two per cluster. If the branch looks weak, prop it up using a wooden stake with a forked head. Try to cushion the area between the branch and the stake with soft material or rubber – sections of tyre work well.

Thinning grapes is also a June pastime. You need to shorten the trusses but leave the shoulders of the bunches intact. Cut up into the bunch, removing most of the interior grapes and any very small ones. There are special long-bladed scissors for this and generally two pairs are used. The technique is not to touch the fruit, but only the stems. After thinning, inspect the fruit every week, cutting out any split or diseased grapes.

Did you know? The earliest descriptions of fruit-thinning appear in 1771 in a book about vines. The process was carried out with great precision. A long, pencil-like stick was used to separate the bunches of grapes and the gardener would then snip and shape the bunches. The thinnings were taken to the kitchen to be made into tarts and pies, or they were juiced.

Organic Tip ✔

When thinning apples, look for the 'king apples' at the centre of each cluster. These are generally misshapen and often have no stalk. Remove them before thinning the rest of the cluster, as getting rid of this 'cuckoo' produces bigger fruit.

JUNE

Think of June as a summer aperitif before the real banquet begins. Savour the moment and enjoy those long days before the summer solstice. You will devour your first home-grown strawberry this month and it will taste entirely different from the hard, commercial varieties picked when under-ripe. You may already have eaten your first acid-green gooseberry fool and you can see the apples, pears and plums filling out before your very eyes.

Strings of currants begin to glisten now. Redcurrants are the most translucent of all, epitomizing high summer. If you're new to fruit-growing, arm yourself with a good jam-making pan!

1 Summer-prune Gooseberries

(early June)

THE AIM in fruit-growing is to produce flowering buds and generally this is achieved by shortening the long laterals in winter to
promote bushy growth. By summer these bushy growths are long,
so now you need to shorten the side shoots on fruit trees and
bushes to concentrate their energy into producing flowering buds
on short spurs. This is important with gooseberries for many
reasons. Firstly it makes the bush less congested, allowing more
air to penetrate, and this helps to prevent mildew. Secondly,
your fruit will be bigger and better because there is less wood.
Thirdly, gooseberries, which are one of the most fecund fruits,
can over-crop and exhaust themselves and this may leave them
vulnerable to disease.

Summer-pruning consists of reducing the young side shoots
back to five leaves: these are easy to see now because this year's
wood is light brown. This approach suits cordons, fans, bushes and
standards.

Cordons and fans need to be kept in strict shape, so you must
remove any deviant wood that does not conform to the trained
shape.

Bushes should also be thinned, with all low branches cut away
so that they develop a short trunk – about 22cm (9in) in height.

Standard gooseberries must be pruned so that they are kept to
a minimal shape. If you allow the top to get too bushy or too large
it can snap at the graft in a heavy summer gale.

Did you know? The first gooseberry bushes written about were imported into England from France in 1275 and were planted in Edward I's garden at the Tower of London. Henry VIII was also a fan and imported bushes in 1509. Royal patronage meant that by the end of the seventeenth century gooseberries were being widely grown. Many varieties were bred in the late eighteenth and early nineteenth centuries by British nurserymen and one, 'Hero of the Nile', was named to commemorate Nelson's victory at the Battle of the Nile in 1798.

Organic Tip ✔

Gooseberry sawfly grubs can strip bushes in early summer. However, on many occasions friendly chaffinches and blue tits gather the grubs up for their young. Avoid spraying for this reason.

SECRETS OF SUCCESS

- Pruning now promotes growth because the sap is racing away and the light and warmth are at their best. Very vigorous varieties – for example, 'Winham's Industry' and 'Howard's Lancer' – can over-respond and for this reason should be pruned only lightly.
- With old, congested bushes of all varieties, cut out some old, gnarled branches to open up the shape.
- Shortening the lateral back to five leaves often solves aphid problems, as they tend to feed on the new growth.

2 Prune Grapes
(early June)

GRAPE-GROWING is tricky in many of the parts of the UK because we are pushing them to the edge of their range and beyond. However, the warm slopes of the Sussex Downs, areas of Surrey and Kent, and the sheltered Leadon Valley in Gloucestershire are places where vines do grow well in the open. In fact, now that autumns are lasting longer, there are 400 vineyards in England, producing 2 million bottles of wine a year. If you want to dabble in wine-making it may be worth growing outdoor grapes, provided you have a sunny slope and lighter soil. Most of us, sadly, do not have enough room for our own vineyard, but you could aspire to grow one vine for edible grapes.

Grapes need pruning and training or they will produce all leaf and very little fruit. The simplest training method is the rod-and-spur system. A strong vertical is trained and side shoots develop close to the main stem. These are then trained and tied along strong wires. This is the system most often used under glass and against walls outside. Vines grown in open ground are trained using the double Guyot system. With either system, all the serious pruning of grapes takes place in winter when the sap is not running (see page 161). Now is the time to prune the flush of spring extension growth and to restrict the amount of fruit. Vines under 3 years old should not be allowed to produce fruit. Remove any that you see.

In the rod-and-spur system, the main stem – the rod – is pinched out when it reaches the desired height – usually 3m (10ft) or less. In spring the two fat buds to which each lateral – or spur – was cut back in winter grow away strongly. The strongest – the 'heir' – is allowed to grow and fruit; the weakest – the 'spare' – is cut back to a couple of leaves. Now, in June, summer-pruning consists of shortening the small leafy growths. Those without flower are pruned back to five or six leaves. Those with flower trusses are cut back to two leaves after the truss. Allow just one cluster to develop per lateral shoot for the best dessert grapes. Tie in the pruned growth loosely to allow for regrowth. You may need to prune the regrowth later.

Bunches may need to be thinned to prevent overcrowding; use a pair of long, thin scissors. Remove all developing grapes that face inwards and thin outward-facing grapes so that those left can plump up nicely for eating.

For open-ground vines, pruned according to the double Guyot system, the three central replacement shoots are tied in vertically but not pinched out. The fruit-bearing laterals are also trained vertically but are pinched out three leaves above the top wire.

Did you know? Vines have an ancient history. We know that wine was made by the Egyptians from vines growing in the Nile Delta almost 5,000 years ago. Paintings in the tomb of the astronomer and scribe Nakht (c.1400 BC) depict vine-growing, with bunches of grapes being trodden by men steadying themselves with ropes.

Organic Tip ✔

Even if you fail to grow edible grapes successfully, a vine on a pergola is a great addition to any garden. The dappled shade cast by the large leaves is perfect for sitting under, and the leaves colour up wonderfully in autumn. The blackbirds are very glad of any small fruit produced.

SECRETS OF SUCCESS WITH GRAPES

- A sunny position and good drainage are vital, so a south-facing slope is the ideal. Cool greenhouses and sheltered walls can also be used.
- Take time to prune and train your vine.
- Restrict the fruit and thin the trusses with grape scissors.

VARIETIES

'Black Hamburgh' (now known as 'Schiava Grosso')
This needs an unheated greenhouse to produce its reliable crops of flavourful black grapes. Widely grown and good to eat.

'Buckland Sweetwater'
An easy, pale-green grape that produces early trusses in abundance. Best under glass and not too vigorous, so suitable for a small greenhouse. May need extra feeding.

'Interlaken'
For a wall or fence. Medium-sized, golden fruit. Thin the bunches for the optimum crop. Good in a cool climate.

'King's Ruby'
Large bunches of dark-purple–mauve grapes with a rich flavour. For the greenhouse or a warm wall.

3 Peg Down Strawberry Runners

(mid-June)

SOME STRAWBERRY varieties produce runners and these will be coming thick and fast now. You should allow only strong, established plants to form runners. If the mother plant is small or very young, cut them away. Plants often bear more than one runner on each stem, but it is best to trim them back to just one runner to conserve the mother plant's energy if you wish to keep that plant for next year. If you are scrapping that plant, you can allow it to run itself out to exhaustion.

Runners can either be potted up into small pots (whilst still attached to the mother plant) or pegged down. The easier of the two is to peg them down into the soil, because then they are largely self-sufficient and need less care. If the weather is hot, small potfuls can shrivel and dry. Lengths of bendy, green-coated wire, readily available from garden centres, are the best material for pegging down, or you can just weigh the runner down with a stone.

Once the runners have rooted well, cut them off from the mother plant and either pot them up or plant them in a new bed straight away.

Keep the young plants well watered. Always resist the urge to let spare runners root into your strawberry bed among your established plants. This will result in a poorer crop.

Keep a look out for vine weevil: the telltale signs are semi-circular notches on the edges of the leaves. If you see this, give all your plants a good tug. Any badly affected ones will come away in your hand. Bin them. Use vine weevil nematodes immediately.

Did you know? Strawberries have been a popular food for centuries, but at first they were the wild strawberries from *Fragaria vesca*, which produces tiny red fruits in woodland and hedge bottoms. People used to dig up the roots and plant them in their own gardens. They were used medicinally as a treatment for fever, rheumatism and gout, and the leaves were used as a tea substitute. They are a good source of vitamin C. Fruit was rubbed on to the skin to lighten freckles and soothe sunburn, and they were also used to whiten the teeth.

Organic Tip ✔

Strawberries love rich, friable soil, so double digging a strawberry patch when planting new runners will double your crop. Keep the new bed well weeded and fed with potash (liquid tomato food) between early May and late August.

SECRETS OF SUCCESS

- If you want to produce lots of runners to bulk up a favourite variety, cut off all the blossom as it appears.
- Strawberries are fairly shallow-rooted, so young plants and runners need to be kept well watered until established.
- Eradicate any weeds from your bed because strawberries resent competition.

4 Train New Blackberry Shoots

(mid-June)

BLACKBERRIES are the perfect partner for cooking apples and they freeze well too, so if you have room, plant one. Thorniness differs from variety to variety, as does stature – see Varieties, page 27. Some can be accommodated in a container while others will fill an entire corner of the garden, though it's quite possible to train them up a fence, over a trellis, or up a pergola. Thornless varieties like 'Oregon' have decorative cut foliage and are suitable for the ornamental flower garden.

Blackberry flowers are extremely attractive to bees and butterflies – they do not need a partner close by to set fruit. However, fruit set is heavier if your blackberry is in a sheltered position.

The more vigorous blackberry varieties send out new runners during the summer and these will replace the older runners that are bearing fruit this year. The new runners can be treated in various ways. Some gardeners tie them into a bundle in autumn, then untie and arrange them in early spring; others train them in now on stout wires – see page 25. In both cases the old runners are cut out at the base once they have finished fruiting. This encourages vigour.

Did you know? The British blackberry is not a single species but a complex group of 350 micro-species. Some areas have micro-species that have large fruit; others have mean little berries. If you find a good bush, make a note of where it is.

Organic Tip ✔

Blackberries propagate by tip-rooting. If you want a new blackberry, just bury the tip of one branch into the soil. It will root with alarming speed.

SECRETS OF SUCCESS WITH PRUNING BLACKBERRIES

- Equip yourself with strong leather gloves, goggles and long sleeves before doing battle with a thorny blackberry.
- Use sharp loppers and reduce the canes in stages — it's safer (see page 27).
- Pruning encourages vigour, so make it a yearly event.

VARIETIES

For varieties of blackberry, see February, page 27.

5 Look After Your Citrus Fruit

(*late June*)

ORANGES were once the height of fashion for rich landowners – so much so that special orangeries were built to accommodate them. In winter the oranges were kept warm inside, but in summer the trees were taken outside because the heat of the orangery became too intense for them. This is a good system to adopt even if you do not have your own orangery.

Keeping citrus in good condition needs a careful hand and constant vigilance. They like a gentle regime free from extremes and are not plants for the weekend or casual gardener. At this time of year your orange or lemon tree should go outside. Find a warm, sheltered place away from scorching sun and stand your pot on a tray of wet pebbles. This will help to promote humid air and prevent die-back and leaf drop. Do not allow your tree to dry out. In hot weather, a daily water is advisable and rainwater can be sprayed on the leaves as well. Their love of humidity makes citrus poor houseplants for centrally heated homes, although they can do well in heated conservatories with ventilation.

Fruit ripens over winter, but all leafy growth takes place in summer, so a nitrogen-rich citrus food should be used; special winter and summer formulas are available. Most citrus fruit is trained as a mop-headed tree and summer-pruning consists of pinching back any branches that seem to be growing too strongly in order to maintain this rounded shape. If you need to remove a branch, February or March are the best months.

Did you know? Satsumas are the hardiest citrus of all, able to survive -11°C (12.2°F) for short periods. The variety 'Owari' proved to be the hardiest citrus in a recent trial, surviving several nights when temperatures fell to -6°C (21.2°F) and below. The British citrus expert Martin Page finds that his specimen 'produces a small crop of edible fruit, without fail, every year'.

SECRETS OF SUCCESS

- A young tree will grow much quicker without fruit for the first year, but after that clusters of fruit should be thinned so that each 1m (3ft) tree bears up to twenty fruits.
- Lemons are easier to grow than oranges, but both are tender plants that must be protected from frosts. Night-time temperatures must be at least 11°C (52°F): this will allow the lemon tree to flower and produce fruit throughout the year. This needs to be maintained through winter if possible. Ideally, day temperatures should be 3°C (10°F) higher than this in order to encourage the fruit to ripen.
- Re-pot in late spring if needed, either into the same pot or a slightly larger one. Remove the top couple of inches and tamp in new compost. Use John Innes No. 2 for smaller plants and No. 3 for larger specimens. Add horticultural grit or perlite for extra drainage.
- When watering, allow some water to run out of the pot; this helps to prevent the build-up of harmful salts in the compost.

Organic Tip ✔

Even if your citrus is growing happily in a greenhouse or conservatory, it is still a good idea to move it outside for the summer, because predators (like ladybirds) will be able to frisk the foliage.

VARIETIES

'Improved Meyer'

This is the easiest lemon. The original 'Meyer' was named after the American botanist who brought it back from China in 1902, but it was found to be a symptomless carrier of citrus tristeza virus, a serious disease. 'Improved Meyer' is the virus-free form and should be the one you grow. It reaches 120cm (4ft) and fruits prolifically through most of the year. A cross between a lemon and a mandarin, so not as acidic as many lemons. Foliage is very large.

'La Valette'

A cross between a lime and a lemon, but the fruit is the same shape and size as lemon. Crops well. Compact and easy.

'Quatre Saisons' (syn. 'Gary's Eureka', or just 'Eureka')

Fragrant citrus flowers and fruit through all four seasons. A true lemon that produces lots of fruit. A favourite with many. Can grow large.

'Imperial'

Thought to be a grapefruit x lemon hybrid, it bears much larger fruit than other lemon trees, but fewer of them. Vigorous.

JULY

This is a month for harvesting soft fruit and for summer-pruning. Many fruit trees get a second burst of growth in July and many laterals put on leafy growth on their side shoots. Apples and pears, which are spur-fruiting, need this new wood shortened to encourage more fruiting buds to form knobbly spurs.

Stone fruits tend to suffer from fungal and bacterial diseases, therefore radical pruning should be carried out now, when flowing sap can heal the wounds quickly, rather than in winter, when disease might enter through the cut. Apricots, however, are less prone to disease and can be pruned in early spring.

1 Look Out for Woolly Aphids

(early July)

KEEP AN eye out for woolly aphids on your apple trees. These brown-black pests produce a waxy white fluff that almost looks like mould. It can appear from late spring onwards and usually persists until early autumn. At first the aphids live in cracks and crevices on the bark, and sometimes on pruning cuts. They feed on the tree sap to begin with, but then they move to soft new growth. In extreme cases the trees develop soft, lumpy growths that are very visible in winter; these are caused by the chemicals secreted into the plant as the aphids feed. These bumpy lumps tend to split in frost and this is when apple canker can take hold. You can buy canker paint and badly affected trees may be improved by pruning, but this will depend on where the lumps are – with cordons and espaliers they often develop on the trunk.

Woolly aphids themselves won't travel to other plants, so it's a very good idea to try to combat them now before they develop into winged adults and move on to new host plants. They are extremely difficult to get rid of because they tuck themselves under bark. There are biological controls, but I prefer the organic 'hands-on' method. Now is the time to scrub them off with a stiff brush, or you can hose them off. This lessens the numbers and limits the damage. Also, in a healthy, spray-free garden there should be plenty of natural predators waiting to pounce. Lacewings are excellent predators of pests in trees.

Did you know? Woolly aphids overwinter on their host plants as immature nymphs. They hide in cracks in the bark or in crevices around old feeding areas. There is no telltale white fluff in winter.

Organic Tip ✔

Bacterial canker is a serious fungal disease of apples that causes die-back and it mostly starts near pruning scars. Keep an eye out for any dead wood, removing and destroying it as soon as you see it.

SECRETS OF SUCCESS

- Remove any infected soft shoots showing the character-istic white fluff produced by aphids now and burn or destroy them.
- Always use sharp secateurs, loppers and pruning saws. Wash them after use, then sterilize them with boiling water, or bleach them, between trees.
- If removing a limb, cut into the bottom of the trunk before making the cut from above, to give yourself a clean cut. Get a helper if it's a large limb.
- Always try to cut into clean, white wood where possible.
- If you have exposed a large area, apply wound paint.
- If you spot dead wood, prune it out and destroy it. It may be canker and special canker paint can be applied.

2 Summer-prune Pears and Apples

(early July)

PEARS ARE not such reliable croppers as apple trees in the British climate. They need warmth in the weeks following pollination to encourage pollen-tube development, which enables the fruit to form. They also like more moisture than apples. Although we can provide extra water, warmth is in the lap of the gods. However, by July your pear crop should be developing well if the fruit managed to set in the first place. Thin the fruit if the tree is still laden after the natural June drop – see page 85. Sharp scissors are the best weapon. Aim for two fruits per cluster as less thinning is needed for pears than apples.

The new growth will be obvious by July. Summer-pruning of pears and apples is basically the same as in winter, although the shape of the trees often differs. It consists of shortening the leading branches back to five or six leaves. Then the laterals (the side shoots off the main branches) that you winter-pruned (see pages 10 and 12) are cut back to one leaf, although you will have to work round the crop. New lateral shoots developed this year are cut back to two or three leaves.

Did you know? Pears like heavy soil and the best pear-growing areas are often close to rivers. Waterperry near Oxford, obviously a pear-growing area for centuries, lies low down by the river where the air is kept mild by the flowing water, which acts as a storage heater. When wine was in short supply in the Napoleonic Wars, sparkling perry became the preferred tipple.

Organic Tip ✔

Pears produce their blossom early and spring frosts often prevent a crop. If you have a warm slope, plant your pear there. The frost should slide down to the bottom of the slope and miss your blossom. Like apples, pears are divided into four pollination groups and if you have a cold garden you should plant those in Pollination Group D, sometimes called the late group.

SECRETS OF SUCCESS

- If your garden is cool, opt for 'Conference' – a self-fertile pear with elongated fruit that wants to crop heavily.
- Some pears are self-fertile but many need a partner in the same pollination group. Pears are not as widely grown as apples, so you will almost certainly have to plant two varieties yourself rather than relying of pollen from neighbouring trees.

VARIETIES

For varieties of pear, see January, page 15, and September, page 130. For varieties of apple, see January, page 11, and September, pages 129 and 133.

3 Plant and Summer-prune Kiwifruit

(mid-July)

THIS IS a good time to plant a kiwifruit and also the time to prune an established one. However, I live in the cold heart of the country and I have never managed to raise one edible fruit despite having had a vigorous self-fertile plant that rambled very prettily over a shed for 10 years or more. It shrugged off cold winters – kiwis are actually hardy to −8°C (18°F) – but it never produced any flower or fruit.

If you have a warm, sheltered garden in good, bright light, you are much more likely to succeed. Kiwi plants are mainly dioecious, however: they have either male flowers with feathery, egg-yolk-yellow-tipped anthers, or female flowers with pure-white middles and strong stigma. Some modern varieties are self-fertile and these are popular because you need only one plant.

The key to getting fruit is correct summer-pruning to restrict the rampant growth. The flowers should appear in early summer along the length of one-year-old wood and at the base of new shoots. Once the framework of branches has been established, cut back the fruiting shoots to five or six leaves. This diverts the plant's energies into producing fruit buds and, with less leaf, the developing fruit is exposed to sunlight. Fruit-bearing shoots can be cut to five or six leaves past the kiwifruit. There is no need to thin the fruit.

After the fruit has been harvested, those shoots need to be shortened back to 5–7.5cm (2–3in) in length to encourage more fruit buds.

Did you know? The kiwifruit, *Actinidia deliciosa*, is native to southern China, not New Zealand. Cultivation spread from China in the early twentieth century when seeds were introduced to New Zealand by Isabel Fraser, the principal of Wanganui Girls' College, who had been a visiting missionary in China. The seeds were planted in 1906 by a Wanganui nurseryman, Alexander Allison, and the first New Zealand fruit was harvested in 1910. People who tasted it thought it had a gooseberry flavour, so it was called the Chinese gooseberry. It did not become known as kiwifruit until *c.*1960, when New Zealand growers thought the furry brown fruit resembled their national bird, the kiwi. Italy is now the leading producer, followed by New Zealand, Chile, France, Greece, Japan and the United States.

SECRETS OF SUCCESS

- Buy well-grown plants with a strong main stem and space them 3m (10ft) apart. If they are not self-fertile, plant a male and a female.
- Plant them in good light in an open, sunny position.
- Kiwifruit need well-drained, moisture-retentive soil, so prepare the ground well when planting.
- Summer moisture swells the fruit, so water well in the growing season. Mulching helps once spring warms up, but avoid contact with the main stem.
- Feed with a high-potash feed in late winter, then use a general fertilizer.
- Cold, wet soil damages the roots in winter, so those on clay soil will have great problems.

> ### *Organic Tip* ✔
>
> *This is a fruit for a warm garden! It needs a long growing season in order to ripen well. If you can grow it, and then eat it, it will boost your vitamin C levels enormously.*

VARIETIES (NB ONLY FEMALE OR SELF-FERTILE PLANTS BEAR FRUIT)

'Hayward'
The most widely grown female kiwi. It is very late-flowering and produces large, broadly oval fruits with good flavour.

'Tormuri'
This late-flowering male cultivar is suitable for pollinating 'Hayward' (above).

'Jenny'
A self-fertile variety, it can produce well-flavoured fruits.

'Issai'
This hardy kiwi belongs to a different species, *A. arguta*. It bears small fruits about the size of a grape in July or August. These are eaten whole.

4 Order New Apple Trees for Autumn Dispatch

(late July)

THIS IS an excellent time to think about ordering new fruit trees and bushes because specialist nurseries will be producing stock for autumn and winter delivery. At this time of year the choice is greatest and because popular varieties sell out quickly, it's worth making decisions and buying now. Ask the nursery to send them out in the fruit-planting season, not in summer.

Nursery stock is either container-grown or bare-root and often both are available. On most soils the container-grown tree is best planted in early September. The ground is still warm and the days still clement, so a newly planted tree will settle in before next spring. However, if you garden on clay soil my advice would be to wait until spring, because heavy soil is wet and cold in winter. You could also improve the ground by adding organic matter or coarse grit. Another technique, often used by Victorian gardeners, is to plant on a raised mound so that the water has somewhere to drain away.

Bare-root trees are sent out when dormant and can arrive between November and March. If you order now you will be at the top of the list and should get your trees in November. Prepare the ground before planting and cover it up with cardboard or old carpet to keep out the frost, so that when your tree arrives you can plant it out on the first clement day.

For general advice on planting, see page 4.

Did you know? Lots of rootstocks were used by our ancestors, but the naming was very muddled. For example, as many as fourteen different kinds of rootstock were all labelled 'Paradise'. In 1912 Ronald Hatton and Dr R. Wellington of the East Malling Research Centre in Kent began to sort out the incorrect naming. In 1917 the John Innes Centre, then based at Merton near London, joined with East Malling and they began a breeding programme to produce better rootstocks. The Malling–Merton series is still used with apples today – see Types of Apple Rootstock, opposite. 'MM' means that the rootstock came out of the collaboration and a single 'M' denotes that the rootstock was developed at East Malling.

TYPES OF APPLE ROOTSTOCK

MM111 – vigorous

Suitable for a wide range of soils and staking not necessary if one-year-old trees are planted. The mature height is 5m (15ft) and the yield at maturity is 45–180kg (100–400lb) of fruit. Fruit appears after 3–4 years. Used on standard, half-standard and large espalier apples.

MM106 – semi-vigorous

Suitable for a wide range of situations and soils – even poor soil. Trees reach an average of 3–4m (10–13ft)) with a spread of up to 4m (13ft). Stake for the first 5 years. Fruit is produced after 3–4 years and the yield at maturity is 23–56kg (50–100lb). Used on half-standard, bush, cordon, espalier and container.

M26 – semi-dwarfing

Can be grown in all reasonable soil conditions, including grassy orchards. Stake for the first 5 years. Trees reach an average of 2.4–3m (8–10ft) when mature, with a spread of 3.6m (12ft). Fruit is produced after 2–3 years and the yield at maturity varies between 13.5–36kg (30–80lb). Planting distance is 2.4–3.6m (8–12ft) apart with 4.5m (15ft) between rows. Used on bush, pyramid, centre leader, cordon, minaret, espalier and container. Suitable for small gardens.

M9 – dwarfing

Needs good fertile soil and weed-free ground. Permanent staking is required. Water in dry conditions. Trees reach an average of 1.8–2.4m (6–8ft) with a spread of 2.7m (9ft). Plant 2.4–3m (8–10ft) apart. The yield at maturity will be 11–23kg (25–50lb). Fruit appears after 2 years. Used on bush, pyramid, centre leader and cordon.

M27 – extremely dwarfing

Requires fertile soil conditions and the ground needs to be weed- and grass-free. Permanent staking required. Water in dry conditions. Trees reach 1.2–1.8m (4–6ft) in height with a spread of 1.5m (5ft). Plant 1.2–1.5m (4–5ft) apart with 1.8m (6ft) between rows. The yield at maturity is 4.5–7kg (10–15lb) of fruit, and fruit appears after 2 years. Used on dwarf pyramid, centre leader and stepover apples, but not on weaker-growing varieties.

For varieties of apple, see January, page 11, and September, pages 129 and 133.

SECRETS OF SUCCESS

- Research your local varieties by telephoning the managers of specialist fruit nurseries, going to 'apple days' and to local gardens.
- Don't be too tied up on heritage fruit varieties. Explore the modern too: breeding in North America is producing cold-tolerant varieties that will do well in the UK.
- Prepare the ground well, then stake and tie in the tree as you plant.
- Rootstocks govern the vigour of trees. Apples vary greatly in habit, so do ask about which to grow — your experienced nurseryman will know which varieties do well on which rootstock.

5 Summer-prune Cherries, Plums, Nectarines and Peaches

(late July)

THESE FRUIT trees are not pruned in winter due to silver leaf disease – see page 28. Instead they get sympathetic pruning now so that the sap seals the wounds.

Plums should first have any diseased or dying wood removed. Then, leaving the main leading shoot at the apex of the tree alone, shorten the branch leaders (the growth at the tips of the branches) by 15cm (6in). The side shoots or laterals are cut to three leaves and any sub-laterals (secondary shoots from the laterals) are cut back to one leaf. This maintains the shape of the tree – usually pyramidal.

Peaches and nectarines need very little pruning because they crop on young wood produced in the previous year. New shoots should be retained every 10cm (4in) along the leaders. Do not prune these leaders. However, cut out any other surplus shoots to roughly 2.5cm (1in) to relieve overcrowding.

Cherries are divided into sweet dessert cherries and acid cherries and both are pruned after the fruit has been harvested. Sweet cherries fruit on one- and two-year-old wood and on spurs of older wood. As a result, they require lighter pruning. Remove any dead, damaged or diseased branches. Then remove very weak and badly placed wood. Shorten the tips of the remaining branches by about a third of their new growth to help encourage the development of fruit buds. Cut out any side shoots that are over 30cm (12in) in length and thin out very crowded shoots. Leave side shoots that are less than 15cm (6in) long unpruned. You can shorten other side shoots to five or six buds to encourage a succession of fruit over the next 2 years.

Acid cherries, which produce dark fruit that is usually cooked rather than eaten raw, are more vigorous and are pruned and thinned more rigorously, as they fruit on the previous year's wood. Remove any dead, damaged or diseased branches and any weak or badly positioned branches that are rubbing together. Then remove about a quarter of the remaining older wood, cutting back to a main branch or younger side shoot. This reduces overcrowding and encourages new growth.

Organic Tip ✔

Stone fruit are much easier to net against birds. They are also easier to cover up in winter to prevent disease.

Did you know? The Romans are thought to have introduced the sweet cherry to Britain, and they in turn got it from Turkey in the late first century AD. Archaeologists, though, have found cherry stones in sites all over Europe that date back to 1000 BC and beyond. The wild cherry grows throughout Europe and produces pleasantly edible fruit. What is odd is that some cultivated varieties have an extra chromosome – seventeen instead of the sixteen of the wild cherry. Perhaps the Romans did after all obtain an ancient hybrid from Turkey, which is still the world's largest producer of cherries today.

SECRETS OF SUCCESS WITH STONE FRUIT

- Look for modern varieties resistant to peach leaf curl (see page 70).
- Seek out the dwarfing cherry rootstock Gisela 5. Trees and fans will reach 3m (10ft) in height when mature. At the moment only 'Stella', 'Sunburst' and 'Morello' (an acid cherry) are available. All cherries grown on any Gisela rootstock need permanent staking.
- Acid cherries (including 'Morello') can produce a crop on shady north-facing or east walls.
- North American and Canadian breeding is producing cold-tolerant varieties, but generally most stone fruits love warmth.

AUGUST

If you've planted an early apple like 'Worcester Pearmain', you'll be crunching strawberry-flavoured apples by now. It's fine to gorge on them because they have a short shelf-life, so I never begrudge the starlings a few. And they will indulge! You'll also have to watch out for wasps: they switch from an insectivorous diet to a sugar-rich one during this month. It goes without saying that I don't approve of traps.

Plums are also part of August's bounty and one of the most accommodating fruits for the British climate – although there are good plum years and bad. Some crop reliably, especially 'Victoria', though there are others with a better flavour. If you have room to grow suitable different varieties, it is possible to pick plums from July until early autumn.

If the fruit falls on the ground, Peacock butterflies will dance attendance on it, but any mummified fruit stuck to the branches should be removed.

1 Thin Summer-fruiting Raspberry Canes

(*early August*)

SUMMER-fruiting raspberries will soon be finishing if they haven't done so already. When they have, it's time to cut down the spent canes at ground level in order to allow the new ones more food and space to develop. Ideally these new canes should be 10cm (4in) apart and any weak canes or very overcrowded ones should be cut out. It's easy to see the difference between the old and new, as this year's will still be light green while last year's now wear a darker patina.

Once your summer-fruiting raspberries have been thinned, feed them with a general-purpose fertilizer and then mulch them with garden compost. You can also use farmyard manure from a reliable source.

Have a good look at the leaves to see whether they are showing signs of chlorosis, or yellowing. If so, the veins will stand out very greenly. It will almost certainly be an iron deficiency and raspberries grown on alkaline soil are especially likely to suffer from this. Apply an iron-rich supplement like Sequestrene 138, using the recommended dose on the bag. If the leaves do not improve, it may be a virus. Unfortunately, raspberries that fall victim to viruses produce stunted canes and little fruit, so prompt action is essential. Dig out affected canes and discard or burn them. Do not put them on the compost heap. There is no other treatment.

If you have room for more canes, growing an autumn-fruiting variety should be an essential because these fruit until late autumn, producing soft fruit when there's little else around.

Did you know? The raspberry is native to almost all parts of Britain except the wet soils of the Fens. It prefers open woodland and scrub, where it often forms extensive thickets. Its seeds are dispersed by birds.

Organic Tip ✔

Summer-fruiting raspberries are more prone to attack by the raspberry beetle than autumn-fruiting varieties. In autumn, dig over your plot to uncover overwintering beetles and larvae so that the birds will find and eat them. If you have chickens, they can help. Mine spend winter in the fruit cage, fertilizing as well as controlling pests.

SECRETS OF SUCCESS

- Once you've cut out the old canes of the summer-fruiting varieties, tie the new ones into the support framework as soon as you can.
- Restrict unwanted canes – they tend to ramble into paths, etc. Chop them out with a spade.

VARIETIES

For varieties of summer-fruiting raspberry, see March, page 53; for varieties of autumn-fruiting raspberry, see February, page 22.

2 Prune Blackcurrants
(*early August*)

ALL CURRANT bushes make excellent foundation planting in a garden and currants contain a lot of vitamin C. Different types, however, need different treatment. Whereas red- and whitecurrants fruit on older wood and so are pruned as the sap rises (see page 41), blackcurrants fruit on new wood and are more vigorous growers, so the technique is to remove two or three of the older, darker stems at the base every year. This can be done when picking the fruit, or shortly afterwards, or you could do it in winter; however, it is far easier to separate the new wood from the old now, because the freshly produced wood is a pale brown while the old wood is darker. In winter it can be more of a challenge to spot the age of the branches. I also think pruning now produces a vigorous response and your bush is more likely to produce stronger branches.

A small pruning saw or loppers will do the job. Identify the darkest wood and cut out roughly three branches right at the base. Many gardeners cut off branches laden with fruit because the currants are much easier to pick on a table than by bending down.

You are aiming (with all currant bushes) to create a strong framework of branches that allows the air to circulate. Once the leaves are off it is possible to examine the shape of the bush and then remove any weak shoots, any shoots that are making the middle congested and any branches that are too low down. A short trunk about 20cm (8in) high is ideal.

SECRETS OF SUCCESS

• For advice on growing blackcurrants, see March, page 39.

Organic Tip ✔

Blackcurrants are hungry plants and they like a nitrogen-rich feed just as spring breaks — see page 39. They are perfect plants to grow if you keep free-range chickens and they greatly benefit from a winter of chicken manure. Your chickens will have to come out of the fruit cage in spring before the leaves emerge, however.

VARIETIES

For varieties of blackcurrant, see March, page 40.

3 Plant Misted-tip Strawberries

(*mid-August*)

MISTED-TIP strawberry plants are a recent innovation for the home gardener, although they have been used by the trade for many a year. They are raised from unrooted runner tips from the mother plant and then are grown under mist – hence the name. They arrive in bundles with bare roots, so they need to be planted quickly. If you can get them in now you should be able to pick a crop next year. They quickly produce strong, healthy plants and first-year yields are up to 100 per cent better than from other types of strawberry (see page 37). This has to be good news for gardeners.

However, putting plants into the ground in August requires care: young plants need to be kept very well watered throughout this month as the weather can be hot and dry.

Misted-tip plants are available right up until late September, but although this is almost certainly a better time to establish them, it is too late for them to produce a full crop the following summer.

Did you know? The strawberry is neither a true berry nor even a true fruit. The true fruits are the tiny little pips held on the surface of the enlarged, red, succulent receptacle. The receptacle is not part of the flower; it is the tip of the flower stalk on which parts of the flower are held.

Organic Tip ✔

You may see some damage to ripe strawberries caused by a medium-sized black beetle. Do not begrudge the strawberry beetle some fruit — it eats slugs too.

SECRETS OF SUCCESS

• For advice on growing strawberries, see pages 23, 36, 55, 72 and 93.

VARIETIES

For varieties of strawberry, see February, page 25, and March, page 38.

4 Prune and Shape Trained Trees

(mid-August)

IF SPACE is in short supply in your garden, restricted trees are the answer. Several shapes are available and they are useful along paths, round edges and close to walls and fences. They mix well with the flower garden and add a formal framework or structure in winter. Although they are unlikely to crop heavily, the fruit that they do produce is often of higher quality than that from full-size trees – and it is easier to pick. Mildew and disease are less of a problem as the air flow is better in a tree that is pruned and trained into a particular shape.

Trained apples and pears are often grafted on less vigorous rootstocks. The strong framework created by training supports short spurs, so all the fruit is close to the framework. Varieties are chosen carefully for their moderate vigour, so the last thing the gardener wants to do is promote a surge of growth. For this reason trained fruit trees are lightly pruned back to their original shape when the tree's sap is beginning to slow down as temperatures cool and day length gets shorter. Make sure you sterilize secateurs between each tree.

Properly trained trees are expensive and, if at all possible, should be personally chosen rather than ordered over the Internet. They are worth the expense because it is a very skilful job to produce a fine fan, or an espalier. Cordons are easier – but still worth buying ready-made. Otherwise you have to spend many years forming the shape.

For the amateur gardener, rubberized Soft Tie wire makes an ideal material for tying in. Simply maintain the tree's original shape. This is made easier by less-vigorous rooting stocks.

Did you know? The word 'espalier' is French and comes from the Italian *spalliera*, meaning something to rest the shoulder against. During the seventeenth century the term referred to the framework supporting the tree, but later it came to be used to describe the tree itself. The practice of growing trees as espaliers became popular in Europe in the Middle Ages, as it allowed fruit to be grown against castle walls and in courtyards.

Organic Tip ✔

Yearly attention is vital with trained trees because an open frame will allow air to circulate. This helps to prevent fungal diseases.

SECRETS OF SUCCESS WITH TRAINED FRUIT

- Buy first-rate trees from a reputable expert fruit nursery and ask them to recommend suitable varieties on the correct rootstocks.
- Use extra-strong galvanized wire and straining bolts for support and for training your tree. Or you could use the self-tensioning Gripple system: this is easier for the amateur to set up.

RESTRICTED TREE SHAPES

Espalier

The most complex way to grow fruit against a wall or on wires. The main trunk has balanced horizontal stems on each side and these are supported on wires. There are usually four well-spaced arms on either side and fruit spurs are encouraged along the length of each.

Cordon

These are usually planted obliquely (i.e. at an angle) because this slows down the sap and makes the tree more fruitful. The fruiting spurs are held along the main stem. Cordons can be planted close together.

Fan

A short trunk supports radiating branches that stretch out to emulate a peacock's tail. Best up against a wall or fence.

Stepover

A low-growing tree for edging paths, supported on a low, strong wire.

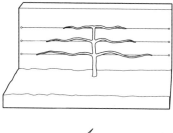

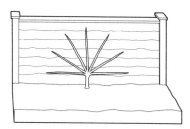

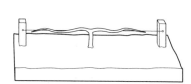

5 Harvest Figs, Cobnuts and Filberts

(late August)

FIGS SHOULD be ripening on the trees now if there has been a good summer. They won't keep, so enjoy them and give any surplus away. Wasps and ants can be a nuisance, so picking in the cool of the early morning, or in the evening, should be less hazardous than during the day. Any figs larger than pea-sized that haven't ripened properly by now should be removed. The pea-sized fruits that remain will develop into your main crop next year, so leave these well alone.

This is also a key time for harvesting hazelnuts – filberts and cobnuts – hopefully before the squirrels descend and strip them from the trees. A good tree can produce 18kg (40lb) of nuts. Try to pick them on a dry day when the husks are just turning yellow. Don't harvest if the husks are still green because the nuts will tend to provide in the shell when stored. Lay your harvested nuts out and, once the husks are dry, store them away somewhere cool where rats and squirrels can't get them, such as a garden shed. A hessian or netting sack is ideal. They will keep throughout the winter.

This is a good time to think about ordering nut trees for September or winter planting. They are easy to grow in a variety of soils, except clay. See page 30 for advice on growing hazelnuts.

Eating hazelnuts is very good for you. They provide fibre, protein, vitamin E, minerals and cancer-fighting antioxidants. They also have a high percentage of unsaturated fats – the good fats that help to keep cholesterol levels down.

Did you know? It is said that the evenly spaced hazelnuts in the nuttery encouraged Vita Sackville-West and her husband Harold Nicolson to buy Sissinghurst Castle in Kent. She first came to see it with her son Nigel in April 1930 when looking for an old house where she could make a new garden. Vita fell in love with Sissinghurst and bought it, along with 400 acres of farmland. The garden is now owned by the National Trust.

Organic Tip ✔

Hazel-leaf litter is highly popular with hibernating insects and small mammals because it's light and dry. Leave it in situ *under the trees and it will rot down to produce friable leaf litter, making it a perfect medium for snowdrops and hellebores.*

SECRETS OF SUCCESS

- Cobnuts and filberts will grow in shade, but they fruit better in good light.
- Try to beat the squirrels to your crop: they have a habit of burying nuts in the lawn and this can cause problems as they scrabble to find them.

VARIETIES

For varieties of fig, see October, page 146; for varieties of cobnut and filbert, see February, page 33.

6 Protect Grapes from Wasps

(late August)

I COULD never condone wasp traps, because wasps are among the most efficient predators in the garden. Our larger wasps – the yellow-and-black ones – are fantastic predators. Almost nothing preys upon the caterpillars of the Cabbage White butterfly because they are full of noxious chemicals, but wasps do. Caterpillars are attacked and killed, cut up and flown piece by piece back to the hive to provide protein for young wasp grubs. As the summer fades, however, wasps switch to feeding on sugary foods like plums, apples and grapes, so the best way to deter them from eating your fruit is to provide plenty of nectar. They adore red hot pokers (*Kniphofia*). The larger, later-flowering pokers such as 'Prince Igor' produce copious nectar at just the right time. (See also Organic Tip opposite.)

Grapes are a particular favourite. If wasps find them they will return time and time again. Deter them by tying any fine-mesh muslin, old net curtains or a commercial soft insect mesh around the ripening branches until the fruit is picked.

Did you know? There are 7,500 species of wasp native to Britain and about 6,000 are parasitoid. This word was coined to describe animals that fit somewhere between predators and parasites. Typically, they lay eggs in their host which hatch into larvae, the larvae consume the host from within, killing it, and then they emerge as adults to repeat the cycle. They are tiny – smaller than their hosts, which include many garden pests such as whitefly and aphids. New species of parasitoids are being discovered all the time.

Organic Tip ✔

*Some of our British native flowers, such as figwort (*Scrophularia nodosa*), specialize in attracting wasps as pollinators rather than bees. A patch of this in an out-of-the-way place will clear the rest of your garden of wasps.*

SEPTEMBER

September is the mellowest month of all. It is now that most apples and pears begin to colour up and ripen, and their sweet aroma can often be detected on warm days. One of the great delights of gardening is to gently twist a sun-warmed, perfectly ripe apple and then sink your teeth into it. It's primeval instinct.

Gardeners do not have to trouble themselves about whether the fruit can travel hundreds of miles in a lorry, or whether it's perfectly shaped and large enough to tempt the supermarket buyer. The odd blemish does not matter either, and the fact that my apples are not chemically tainted is highly important to me. The only consideration is flavour and whether I like it. My 'Pitmaston Pineapple' produces small fruit that some might scorn – but what a flavour! Sweet, with aromatic pineapple overtones. 'D'Arcy Spice' is even better, with its hints of Christmas spice and cinnamon.

1 Harvest and Store Apples
(early September)

GROWING apples should provide a crop that can be stored and, if you intend to do so, they will have to be picked from the tree before they crash to the ground and bruise. They must be full-sized and ripe, and the time-honoured way to tell this is to cup them and give them a twist. Most ripe apples will happily detach themselves from the stem. However, later varieties often need encouragement in the form of a sharp tug – like intransigent children. They are descended from wild genetic material that clings on to its fruit until the following spring, so these varieties rarely detach easily.

Different apples store for different lengths of time, so mark the variety (if you know it) and then add the words 'eat by' to each basketful. For this reason varieties should not be mixed up: if they are, some will rot and spoil the other, longer-lasting types. Apples give off ethylene, a gas, when ripe and this causes fruit nearby to ripen prematurely. Green bananas or an under-ripe avocado placed next to your apples will ripen quickly, so for this reason bananas are normally kept away from apples to prevent premature ripening.

Generally, early-ripening apples keep for 3 weeks at most and are probably best left on a wooden tray somewhere cool. If it's a bumper crop, give some away. Mid-season-ripening fruit keeps for 1–2 months. Late-season fruit (picked in October) will store for the longest of all – between 3 and 8 months. It obviously makes sense to grow at least two late-maturing varieties that can be eaten after Christmas. Don't eat these later apples straight from the tree: they have to be stored to develop flavour and sweetness.

> **Did you know?** Fruit stores traditionally had a soil floor which added a touch of humidity that kept the fruit from shrivelling. A layer of strong mesh wire was usually laid underneath the floor to prevent mice and rats from getting at the fruit. If your store is dry, you may have to dampen it a little by putting out a tray of water.

SECRETS OF SUCCESS

- Apples must be perfectly dry before storage, so pick in the middle of a fine day.
- Look carefully for any breaks in the skin or signs of insect attack. If you're sure the apples are completely sound, carefully place them in a basket (handling them just as you would eggs).
- If you have room, leave them in a ventilated place for 10 days before wrapping, in case they sweat.
- Wrap them in paper or put them in cardboard apple trays, which you can usually acquire from a super-market or fruit stall.
- Wooden orchard trays stack on top of each other and allow the air to circulate, which prevents mould, etc. But an old chest of drawers (with each drawer left slightly open) works too.
- Apples are always stored on their own, well away from pears and other fruit. They pick up taints easily, so you must move strong-smelling tins containing creosote, etc., well away from them.
- A cool, rodent-free garden shed is ideal. Keep the door shut, otherwise birds will soon peck your fruit.
- Check your fruit every month and remove any that show signs of rotting.

Organic Tip ✔

Wrapping stored apples, to ensure the apples never touch each other, prevents a rotten one from infecting the whole batch. The paper barrier keeps the mould spores from escaping. Waxed paper is the ideal, although newspaper has been used for generations. Leave a gap between each wrapped apple. Alternatively use see-through polythene bags so that it is easy to check the apples regularly, removing any that show signs of rot; each bag should store up to 1.8kg (4lb). Make holes in the bags to allow for ventilation. A garage, cellar or outhouse is the perfect place to keep them.

VARIETIES WORTH STORING

'Ashmead's Kernel'
A classic, russet-coloured old English variety. Excellent aromatic flavour, good keeping quality and very attractive blossom. Eat between December and February. Raised in Gloucestershire, *c.*1720. Pollination Group D.

'Bramley Seedling'
Waxy-skinned, large, green cooking apple that cooks to a fluffy purée. Stores really well until March. From Nottinghamshire, 1809 (see page 17). Pollination Group C. A triploid tree with sterile pollen, so grow two more Group C trees to go with it.

'Kidd's Orange Red'
Similar to 'Cox', but redder in colour, sweeter in taste and easier to grow. Eaten between November and January. From New Zealand, 1924. Pollination Group C.

'Blenheim Orange'
A nutty-flavoured old English variety producing large orange fruit streaked in red that can be eaten or cooked. Heavy-yielding with a biennial tendency that is mostly overcome if grown on dwarfing rootstocks. A big triploid tree, so you will need to plant it with two other Group C trees. From Oxfordshire, 1740. Pollination Group C.

For further varieties of apple, see January, page 11, and September, page 133.

2 Harvest Pears
(early September)

PEARS RIPEN rapidly and are entirely different beasts from apples. They don't crop as heavily and they don't store nearly as well. Picked ripe, many develop a 'sleepy' middle, with the centre quickly turning to brown mush. Pears, therefore, are best picked from the tree when ripe: then they will keep in the bottom of a refrigerator (which should stay just above freezing) until November. The one advantage that pears do have over apples is that they can be stored in much cooler temperatures.

When ripe, pears change to a lighter shade of green – that is the time to pick them. They will come away from the stalk and the fruit will have a lovely aroma.

Some heritage varieties can be stored until January, but you need to pick these before they are fully ripe, so check your varieties before planting if you want to store.

VARIETIES FOR STORING

'Passe Crassanne'
A heritage French dessert variety from 1845 with a buttery texture, requiring a warm location – often better against a wall. Stores until February or March. Pollination Group B.

'Packham's Triumph'
An Australian variety from 1896 – effectively a late 'Williams' with yellow, musky flesh. Stores until November. Pollination Group B.

'Winter Nélis'
Not a strong grower, so needs grafting on to Quince A and the small, russet-skinned fruits do require thinning. However, stores until January. From Belgium, 1818. Pollination Group D.

'Glou Morceau'
This buttery 1759 variety from Belgium is the longest-storing pear. Consume between December and January. Crops well, but enjoys sun and warmth. Pollination Group D.

For further varieties of pear, see January, page 15.

Did you know? The most famous British pear variety is the 'Williams', but it wasn't deliberately bred. It arose as a seedling in the garden of a schoolmaster, one Mr Wheeler of Aldermaston in Berkshire, sometime before 1770. It was originally grafted by Richard Williams, a nurseryman from Turnham Green near London, and it took his name. In fact, its correct name is 'Williams Bon Chrétien', meaning 'Williams good Christian'. It is the most widely grown pear in California (where it is known as 'Bartlett's William') and it is the one most often canned.

Organic Tip ✔

Heritage varieties of pear are especially fond of warmth and they should be given the warmest spot possible. Their blossom is frost-hardy, but they need the extra warmth for the pollen tube to grow.

SECRETS OF SUCCESS

- Be realistic! Pears do not store nearly as well as apples.
- Fully ripe pears can be kept in the bottom of the fridge in polythene bags for up to 6 weeks.
- If storing for longer, pick your fruit before it is fully ripe and keep it as cold as possible.
- Lay pears out on wooden or cardboard trays, variety by variety, in an airy place.

3 Grow Later Varieties of Apple

(mid-September)

IF YOU are serious about storing fruit, it's the later varieties of apple that store best. These also tend to flower later and many are good varieties for colder gardens, as the blossom generally misses the frost.

You will still need to avoid frost pockets and plant them in good light so that nectar flow attracts the bees. Plant bare-root trees between November and March; pot-grown trees can be planted throughout the year, but avoid planting in extreme cold or extreme heat. To fruit well apples, pears and plums need cold winters so that they have a full period of dormancy. Given this, they form big, bold, efficient fruit buds. However, the number of chilling hours needed varies according to variety. Sunnier summers also promote bigger fruit buds. The ideal would be a hard winter followed by a warm spring and a sunny summer..

Organic Tip ✔

Ornamental crab apples make excellent pollinators for apples. Possible varieties include 'Golden Hornet', 'Red Sentinel', 'Winter Hornet' or 'Profusion'.

SECRETS OF SUCCESS

• For advice on harvesting and storing apples, see page 127.

> **Did you know?** Summers are getting hotter in England, particularly in the south-east. Because English apples tend to be thin-skinned, with low wax levels on the skin, the fruit can suffer sunburn and can almost cook on the tree. If hot summers persist, varieties with thicker, waxier skins will have to be grown instead. 'Braeburn', bred in New Zealand in 1952, is now widely grown in England for this reason.

RECENT VARIETIES THAT STORE WELL

'Jonagold'
Heavy-yielding apple from the USA, 1943. Fruit is greenish-yellow, streaked in red. Crisp and sweet, with a rich, honey flavour. Stores November–January. Pollination Group D.

'Red Falstaff'
Late, red dessert apple from Kent, 1986. Stores October–December. Pollination Group C.

'Rajka'
Disease-resistant, mid–late red dessert apple from the Czech Republic, 1990s. Stores October–December. Self-sterile. Pollination Group D.

'Pinova'
Late, fruity dessert apple with good disease-resistance from Germany, 1986. Stores November–January. Pollination Group C.

4 Harvest Quinces and Medlars

(mid-September)

QUINCES and medlars, both popular fruits for centuries but grown less often today, can also be harvested now. Medlars (*Mespilus germanica*) are not universally popular because the fruit has to 'blet', which means that you eat it in a brown, almost rotten state. It is an acquired taste and the fruits are small. They do, however, make excellent jelly. Medlars also make good specimen trees for the ornamental garden because their white single flowers on the tips of the branches have a pure charm and they come after the apple blossom, thus extending the blossom season. Bright-green leaves follow and then the fruit forms. Pick them now and store them for a few weeks. They are inedible when fresh, so lay them out flat and leave them in a warm place for 4 weeks or so. They become soft and brown and the flesh can be spooned out. Rely on your taste-buds and nose if you leave them longer.

The quince (*Cydonia oblonga*) is really in the same category and mainly used for making jelly. Quinces hang like huge, ugly pears and they are also picked now and left in a bowl to soften a little. They take ages to cook. At blossom time they are extremely ornamental, with huge, apple-blossom-pink flowers that open from scrolled buds. It is my favourite blossom of all. Sometimes the flowers are veined in darker shocking-pink. They love to grow in gardens close to rivers or in the rain-sodden counties of western England.

Both quinces and medlars come from Asia and so will do best in warmer gardens. Both are self-fertile, so you need only one of each. Different rootstocks are available for both. Trees grafted on to Quince C can be kept small, with blossom appearing at eye level.

Organic Tip ✔

All fruit trees are important sources of pollen and nectar for our endangered bees. A quince, or a medlar, extends the flowering season and the bees flock to them.

Did you know? The medlar is commonly known as 'dog's bottom' or 'monkey's bottom' and you can see why when you look. Other descriptions are even ruder. The tree originated in Persia, becoming popular in Britain in the Middle Ages. The 'bletted' fruit was traditionally eaten at Christmas.

SECRETS OF SUCCESS WITH QUINCES AND MEDLARS

- A warm, sunny position is vital for medlars and quinces.
- Quinces need moisture to produce those huge fruits.
- Opinion varies here, but I prefer to harvest medlars and quinces before the first frosts and store them in a warm place.

VARIETIES

Medlar
'Nottingham'
A very ornamental variety with a good architectural shape that sends branches in odd directions. The foliage colours well in autumn.

Quince
'Vranja'
Grown for its exceptional flavour and perfume. Produces large, golden-yellow fruit. A larger tree than the medlar 'Nottingham'.

5 Pick and Plant Walnuts
(late September)

WALNUTS are so nutritious and high in vitamin E and the 'good' fats that lessen cholesterol that every gardener with room and a suitable site should aspire to grow them. With luck some nuts will survive the annual invasion of agile squirrels swinging Tarzan-like through the branches. Walnuts are not normally picked, but gathered from the ground on a daily basis. The husks, which usually split at this stage, need to be removed because they blacken and go mouldy if left. They can also taint the nut inside. Stored nuts are then kept and dried out so that they lose their wet texture and develop their oily flavour. They are ready to eat when dry to the touch. This usually takes a few weeks.

Some people like to pickle walnuts, but for that they must be picked from the tree while very young, before the shells have begun to develop – usually in July or August.

It is important when starting out to buy a young grafted tree. This will fruit after 4 years, whereas an ungrafted tree could take 20. Plant it in the autumn or during the winter rather than in the spring. British springs and summers can be dry and the walnut is used to an Asian rainy season that produces a heavy summer deluge in the growing period. Spring-planted walnuts seem to get a growth check unless there's a wet summer.

If you have room plant at least two, because although some varieties are self-fertile, the yield is greater if cross-pollination occurs. Walnuts are wind-pollinated, but even compact forms need to be up to 10m (30ft) apart.

Did you know? Walnut husks stain the skin and clothing, so wear old clothes and gloves when handling them. Hard pruning is not tolerated and regular pruning is not necessary. However, walnut trees bleed freely, so if you do need to do it, tackle the job between midsummer and early autumn when the sap is running slowly.

Organic Tip ✔

Walnuts are warm-position trees from Asia and they do not crop well in more northerly latitudes of Britain. Before you plant one, do some local research.

SECRETS OF SUCCESS WITH WALNUTS

- Find a warm, sunny position away from frost. Both flowers and the growth tips can be spoiled by frost.
- Provide deep, fertile soil – heavy loam over limestone is ideal. Avoid water-logged positions.
- Handle the roots carefully when planting and never plant a pot-bound tree.
- Stake your tree when you plant it.
- Keep your tree well watered in dry springs and summers until it is established.
- Don't prune your tree.
- Apply a balanced fertilizer in late February and again in late March. Then add a mulch of well-rotted compost around the base of the tree to retain moisture.

VARIETIES

'Broadview'

This Canadian variety has become the best all-round walnut for UK conditions. It is suitable for smaller gardens and forms a compact, spreading tree. It produces nuts after 3–4 years. The flowers are also quite frost-hardy and it flowers later than most.

'Franquette'

Raised in the heart of Europe's finest nut-growing region around Grenoble in France, this grafted tree produces sweet, moist nuts with a high oil content. Cropping should begin within as few as 3–4 years.

OCTOBER

October days are misty and crisp and there's still fruit to be picked on good, sunny days. Elsewhere the year is winding down and the leaves are turning warm shades of yellow and orange before dropping. The first frosts are beginning to bite, but your fruit will sustain you as the temperatures fall – whether it's stored in shed, freezer or jam jar.

On the work front there's little to be done this month – it's often a lazy month – but October afternoons can still be generously warm. Enjoy it – we are on the cusp of great changes and in a few weeks' time winter will be upon us.

1 Prepare Ground for Bare-root Fruit

(early October)

THERE ARE several advantages to buying a field-grown bare-root tree or bush rather than a container-grown one, including the fact that a bare-root specimen is often cheaper. Also, the range of varieties is greater and some rarer types can be bought only in this way. If you've ordered bare-root fruit trees or bushes, use one of these mellow October days to prepare and enrich the ground so that when they do arrive the chore of planting them on a raw day is all the quicker.

Dig over the ground and weed it well, then add organic matter. This could be garden compost or well-rotted manure from a reliable source. However, all manure must smell sweet (not of ammonia) and be well rotted, otherwise it will scorch the roots. There have been widespread problems with contamination of manure caused by a herbicide called aminopyralid, which has been used on grass fields that have then been cut for silage. When this is fed to cows, the manure coming out of the other end is effectively a herbicide too. So if you do use manure, check to make sure that your farmer hasn't used either the herbicide itself or bought-in silage. If he has, avoid the manure.

Once the ground is fully prepared, cover it up with a double layer of horticultural fleece or old carpet; this will keep the cold and frost out of the soil. When your plants do arrive you will be able to drop them into the ground easily.

Did you know? Bare-root planting is very effective on poorer soils in the drier, eastern half of the country. These conditions are challenging for container-grown plants, particularly if the compost they are in is peaty. Once a peaty root ball dries out it is impossible to rehydrate it. Planting bare-root means you can add nutrients and organic matter (which holds air and water) and put your plant into the ground when dormant. If you keep it well watered in its first two or three growing seasons (April until late August), it will romp away. Bare-root trees are also cheaper to buy, and postage and packing is minimal.

SECRETS OF SUCCESS WITH BARE-ROOT TREES AND BUSHES

- Open the bag as soon as your tree arrives and check the contents.
- Plant as soon as possible – preferably in prepared ground.
- Do not plant in frosty conditions. Keep the bag in a cool, frost-free place, and if the roots look dry, add damp white paper kitchen towels to keep them moist. Alternatively, dig a V-shaped trench, then unpack the plants and lay them in halfway up the stems.
- Long roots can prove difficult when planting. Don't make a hole to fit the roots. Trim long roots back instead and then spread them out. The exception is the tap-rooted walnut (see page 136). Carefully back-fill, then lightly tread in the tree or bush.
- Trees are often grafted, but it's possible to see where the tree left the ground by looking at the trunk – just replant to that level. Order a stake with every tree.
- Water well.
- For further advice on planting, see January, page 4.

2 Take Hardwood Cuttings of Gooseberries and Currants

(early October)

GOOSEBERRIES and currants are very easy to raise from hardwood cuttings at this time of year, although they do take their time to root. It will probably be this time next year before they are ready to move. They callous over in the first winter, then may produce roots in spring – lift them carefully during the following autumn to check. If rooted, either pot them up or move them to their final position; if there are no roots, give them longer – they will probably produce roots in the following spring. Very few cuttings fail.

Plant with the lowest bud 5cm (2in) above the ground, so that the currant or gooseberry bush will have a small trunk and bushy top. Rooting is most successful in a sheltered position and one of the best places is against a northern wall, or on the shady side of a hedge. Gardeners on heavy soil should line a trench with sand to aid rooting, though some prefer hormone rooting powder.

Gooseberries, redcurrants and whitecurrants can be trained as cordons and fans, and can produce a crop on a north-facing wall.

Victorian gardeners would grow a preciously early crop on a south-facing wall, followed by a later one on a north wall.

You can also raise figs and mulberries in this fashion.

Did you know? The jostaberry is a hybrid between the blackcurrant and gooseberry. It is thornless, with dark fruits that resemble gooseberries. These large bushes take 5 years to fruit and are not widely grown, although they make excellent jam. The jostaberry was developed in Germany and commercially released by the Max Plank Institute in Cologne in 1977. The 'josta' name comes from the German words for blackcurrant and gooseberry – *Johannisbeere* and *Stachelbeere*.

Organic Tip ✔

If you do not have too many cuttings, raise them in a large container of gritty compost, but keep them in the shade.

VARIETIES

For varieties of gooseberry, see January, page 10; for varieties of blackcurrant, see March, page 40.

3 Protect Figs for Winter
(mid-October)

FIGS ARE sumptuous plants, but they come from much warmer climates than we enjoy in the UK. However, the National Collection holders (Reads Nursery in Norfolk, www.readsnursery.co.uk), with the help of their customers, have been researching which cultivars are the hardiest. My own very cold, windswept village (its name even begins with Cold!) harbours many thriving 'Brown Turkey' fig trees in the open ground. They crop well in warm summers, but always produce some fruit, whatever the weather.

Many gardeners grow figs in containers that can be moved into a frost-free position for winter, but if you do this make sure they are standing on pot feet to allow any winter wet to drain away. You can keep them in a greenhouse from August until late April; however, if a greenhouse is not available, a garage or garden shed will do between December and March – a shorter time, because a shed is much darker than a greenhouse. Keep the soil just moist and then pot on in March to a size about 5–7.5cm (2–3in) larger in diameter. Use John Innes No. 3. Winter protection is advisable for figs planted in the ground – thick fleece is ideal.

Figs can be pruned in late March before growth starts. Cut out any dead wood or die-back to the healthy, white wood. Remove tips of young shoots and any thin, weak branches, just keeping the thick ones which are the fruit-bearers.

In warm climates a fig tree can produce three crops per year. However, in Britain figs planted in the garden will produce one crop each season and those planted in greenhouses will produce two crops in a sunny season. For harvesting figs, see page 119.

SECRETS OF SUCCESS WITH FIGS

- Provide a warm, sunny position and good drainage. Figs are fairly hardy, but the fruit needs warm sun to ripen.
- Restricting the roots – with wooden shuttering or paving slabs placed under the ground, for instance – minimizes the size of the tree and maximizes the fruit crop. Normally the bottom of the containerized box under the ground is left open to aid drainage but it is packed with a 22cm (9in) layer of rubble to stop large tap roots forming.
- Feed your figs with a general fertilizer in spring, then mulch them with well-rotted organic material.
- Once the fruits form, water on a potash-rich tomato feed until August.
- If you have restricted your fig, it may be thirsty. Water it well in the warm summer weather.
- If your fig drops its fruit in June, it is thirsty.

Did you know? Garden figs are parthenocarpic – the fruit develops without being fertilized. They live for centuries. Cardinal Reginald Pole, Archbishop of Canterbury, introduced the 'White Marseilles' variety to Lambeth Palace in 1525 and his trees are still flourishing.

Organic Tip ✔

If you do train your fig on to a south or south-westerly wall, add a stout support system to which you can tie it. Large-leaved fig branches can snap in gales.

VARIETIES

'Brown Turkey'
The most successful fig for cool climates. Reliable and popular, this mid-season variety produces a profusion of large, pear-shaped, dark-skinned fruits with dark red flesh.

'Brunswick'
Another very popular variety for outdoor culture in cool areas due to its hardiness. A mid-season fig bearing large fruits with yellowish-green skin and reddish flesh.

'Rouge de Bordeaux'
A gourmet fig for a very warm, sheltered site, or a conservatory or greenhouse. Deep-purple skin with red flesh.

'White Marseilles' (syn. 'White Genoa')
Attractive, pale-green–white skin with pale, almost translucent flesh. A good variety for growing outdoors.

4 Tidy Your Rhubarb
(late October)

RHUBARB leaves and stems are affected badly by frost and soon turn limp and soggy, it is a good idea to spruce up your rhubarb patch now, ready for winter. Remove or cut away any remaining leaves: they could be sheltering slugs and snails. Tidy up the patch now, and weed it, so that when spring comes you can enjoy the cooked stems of young rhubarb

You can force rhubarb crowns growing in the ground by covering them with purpose-made terracotta forcers or upturned dustbins full of straw. The dark, warm conditions inside force the rhubarb into growth a month early, causing it to produce soft, pale-pink stems that have a champagne flavour when cooked. However, once you have forced one crown it must be rested for 2–3 years and allowed to grow away naturally. Some gardeners just discard the crowns they have forced.

The simplest thing is to plant three crowns so that one is recovering from being forced the year before, one is cropping naturally and one is being forced. Then you will have a supply of forced stems every year. However, the yield from forced rhubarb is roughly half that of a plant grown outside.

Did you know? Rhubarb is technically a vegetable, but considered an honorary fruit. It needs a cold period before it can begin growing in the spring. Early varieties need a relatively short cold spell; later varieties a long cold period. If you want an early crop of forced rhubarb, you must choose an early variety.

VARIETIES

'Timperley Early' AGM (early)

So early it's probably better not to force it. The long, slender, pink-red stems have a tart flavour that makes it an excellent crumble-filler. Not a prolific cropper, but a must for all rhubarb-lovers.

'Hawke's Champagne' AGM (early–mid-season)

Delicately thin, long, scarlet stems with a sweet flavour from early spring. An old variety, but easy to grow and ideal for forcing. Attractive appearance.

'Queen Victoria' (mid–late-season)

Colourful, strong red stems, easy to grow and prolific. This heritage variety still holds its own today. Vigorous, forming huge clumps, so perhaps not for smaller gardens.

'Raspberry Red' (mid–late-season)

An old Dutch variety recently reintroduced. Heavy cropper for a sunny, open position. Sweet red stems.

SECRETS OF SUCCESS WITH RHUBARB

- Choose an open, sunny site and prepare the soil by working in plenty of farmyard manure or compost before planting.
- Plant in spring, where possible, placing new crowns 1m (3ft) apart with the buds just below the surface. Don't pull any stems until the second year of growth.
- Never cut rhubarb: the technique is to pull, then twist it very gently from the lower stem.
- Stop harvesting at the end of May to allow the plants to recover.
- If a stressed plant should run to seed, remove the flowering spike straight away. Water, feed and mulch lightly.
- Divide large clumps just as the dome-like buds are breaking dormancy. Lift the whole crown and, using a spade, split it into chunks containing four or five buds. Replant in enriched soil containing garden compost, making sure that emerging buds are just above the ground. Do not pick any stems in the first year or two and always remove flowering spikes.

5 Grease-band Trees
(late October)

THE IDEA of applying grease bands is to prevent wingless insects (mainly wingless female moths) from climbing up the trees from the ground to lay their eggs. You can use them on apple, plum, pear and cherry trees. However, the sticky barriers don't work with Codling Moths, which are the cause of maggoty apples. These fly into the trees in midsummer and you will need pheromone traps to upset them (see page 82).

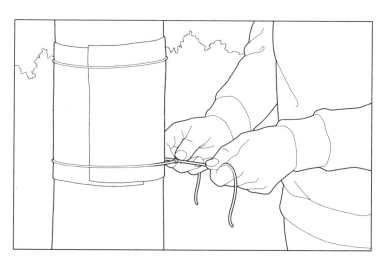

If you have a young tree with a smooth bark, use a ready-prepared sticky paper band – there are many on the market. If you have an old, gnarled apple tree, apply the grease directly to the bark – there are tins of fruit-tree grease and insect barriers on the market too. Place your band or grease about 45cm (18in) above the ground by late October, just before the adult moths emerge in November. Moth activity slows down in January, but wingless females are around until April. Re-apply the grease if needed.

Your grease should trap some of the wingless females before they reach the branches. The Winter moth, *Operophtera brumata*, is the most important. The adults are around between November and mid-January. When the wingless females climb up the tree trunk they make holes in the leaves and eat the blossom and fruitlets, affecting crop yields and quality. In early spring it's possible to see silken threads on the damaged leaves and by midsummer the leaves look very gappy.

The Mottled Umber moth (*Erannis defoliaria*) and March moth (*Alsophila aescularia*) eat leaves and fruit buds between late March and June.

Did you know? Around sixty species of butterfly are seen regularly in the UK, but there are around 2,500 species of moth. A hundred species fly in daylight, but most appear at dusk. They are just as affected by habitat loss as butterflies, with numbers dropping by a third since 1968. Some moths, like the Reddish Buff and Barberry Carpet, are highly threatened. Other species, like the Bordered Gothic, may now be extinct in the UK.

Organic Tip ✔

Don't spray! The tiny caterpillars of these moths form a large part of the diet of baby blue tits. They will clean up many of them. Blue-tit chicks alone feed on an estimated 35 billion caterpillars a year in Britain. The sharp drop in our garden bird populations is almost certainly related to the decline in moth numbers. They are an essential part of the food chain for birds, bats and mammals.

NOVEMBER

November is often the worst gardening month. It can be damp, drear and cheerless, and everything is in decline and decay. However, gardeners appreciate the rest after long hours outside and much planning and taking of stock goes on indoors right up until the shortest day. When thinking about fruit, it's worth noting that there are good and bad fruit years and that different crops do well in some and not in others.

If your top tree-fruit hasn't delivered as well as expected, be an optimist and tell yourself that it will be better next year. Some varieties have a biennial tendency (like the apple 'Bramley Seedling') and they crop abundantly every other year. Don't hold that against them. The satisfaction of having stored fruit to eat is a joy and, as an organic gardener, I love to eat produce from my own patch.

1 Erect Frames Around Peaches, etc.

(early November)

IT IS TIME to cover up peaches and nectarines to prevent peach leaf curl from getting into the buds. It is an airborne disease but, like all fungal diseases, warm and wet conditions encourage it. Putting up sheeting that covers the front of the whole tree from tip to toe will keep off the rain, making it harder for the disease to take hold if it's already present and also preventing new spores from landing on the tree when it's bare. It is the young leaves that are most vulnerable to the fungus: they distort, pucker up and redden, so it is very obvious that the tree is affected. The leaves fall off and then the tree becomes short of food and unfruitful.

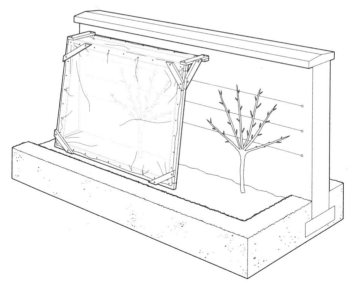

If this does happen, pick off any infected leaves and tidy any from the ground. Continue to do this. Always destroy or bin the leaves – never compost them. Mulch under the tree with bark to form a barrier between any spores on the ground and the tree.

Wall-trained trees are easier to cover up because you can install a pull-down sheet that covers the front whilst allowing air to enter and circulate from the sides. Free-standing trees can have tent-like structures put over them. Polythene is the best material because it isn't porous and it sheds water. It will also warm the area underneath. The sheeting should be kept in place until the fear of frost has passed – until early April is usually sufficient for a wall-trained tree. Lift it up to hand-pollinate your tree (see page 44). Porous fleece isn't a good idea, as a damp membrane exacerbates the problem.

Did you know? The closest relative to the peach is the almond – a ripe almond fruit looks very like a small, unripe peach. It has beautiful but early blossom that is often caught by frosts. Some named varieties of the sweet almond are available in Britain, but nut-set is often poor. If you do get nuts, the shells can be laughably hard – you may need a hammer.

Organic Tip ✔

Peach leaf curl appears most on outdoor-grown peaches; it is rare for a tree under glass to suffer. A seaweed-based feed will toughen up the foliage and make it healthier.

SECRETS OF SUCCESS

• For advice on growing peaches and nectarines, see April, page 68, and July, page 110.

VARIETIES

For varieties of peach resistant to peach leaf curl, see April, page 70.

2 Double Dig for Added Fertility

(early November)

YOUR SOIL is the most important component of your garden and many fruiting plants are long-lived, so the soil should be first rate. Compost heaps will be groaning and some may have fully rotted-down material that can be used in the garden. However, most garden compost heaps are not hot enough to kill off all the weed seeds and inevitably some will be left. Burying your compost underground lessens any weed problems and, whenever the weather is clement, it is possible to double dig areas and add your compost to them.

Double digging is easier to do on smaller areas and it is also much easier than it sounds. You need a groundsheet, a wheelbarrow, a spade and a fork. Lay out your groundsheet on the right if you are right-handed and on your left if you are left-handed. Dig out one spit of soil and pile it on the sheet to reveal a neat area. Then break up the bottom roughly with a fork, to a spade's depth if you can, to improve drainage. Pile your compost 10–15cm (4–6in) high and fork it in. Replace all your topsoil to form a barrow-like mound and allow it to settle. Plant it up in spring.

This fertile mound will double your yield of strawberries, or you can plant fruit bushes.

Did you know? Keeping off your soil is vital. The London market gardeners of the seventeenth century used long beds with paths on either side. Bed width was governed by a man's arm. They were never wider than two arms' lengths so that the gardeners could harvest from either side without having to tread on the ground. The vegetable garden at RHS Wisley has a section devoted to 1.2m (4ft) wide beds.

Organic Tip ✔

When you double dig you are boosting the soil's nutrients, especially nitrogen, but more importantly you are improving the soil structure. This encourages much better root development — and it is the root system that is the most important part of any plant.

3 Repair Wounds and Graft Trees

(*mid-November*)

APPLES and pears can be radically pruned in winter when the sap is not flowing. Peaches, nectarines, cherries and plums are normally only gently pruned in summer when the sap can seal the wounds —

see page 110. However, occasionally large trees may need a damaged limb removing, and then a bitumen-based wound paint is normally applied. The tree will then form its own callus, so you need only treat it with wound paint once.

Care has to be taken when applying it: it could seal in dampness and cause more problems. For this reason opinion on its use is divided. However, most nurserymen and fruit specialists recommend wound paint, and you will certainly have to use it with cherries and plums to prevent disease from entering. Wound paint also prevents frost damage. When a branch snaps, leaving a large surface area, I recommend wound paint.

You can change the variety of apple you grow by over-grafting an established tree with the variety to which you want to change. You need to have scion wood – twigs from your chosen variety. Cut the scion into a 10cm (4in) length and make a slanting cut in it so that there's a 'tongue', or narrow sliver of wood, sticking out. Make a cut into the wood of your living tree, slip the two together and bind with raffia or grafting tape. Cover the join with grafting wax to exclude air. When the graft is successful, the new wood will take over.

Did you know? The Romans were adept at grafting and Roman soldiers were given plots of land to turn into orchards as an incentive to stay in Britain.

Organic Tip ✔

When working on more than one tree at a time, cut down the possibility of cross infection by washing your blades and cutting edges and then sterilizing them in bleach or boiling water. Rinse this off and dry well before cutting into the next tree.

SECRETS OF SUCCESS WITH
CUTTING STEMS AND REMOVING LIMBS

- To cut stems, make the cut just above a healthy bud, or a pair of buds or side shoots. Where possible, cut to an outward-facing bud or branch to avoid congestion in the heart of the plant and to prevent rubbing branches.
- Do not cut too close to the bud, otherwise it may die. However, if you cut too far away you will encourage die-back above the bud and then rots and other infections may enter.
- When removing limbs, wear gloves and eye and head protection.
- Firstly, using a saw, make an undercut about 20–30cm (8–12in) from the trunk. Then saw downwards to prevent the bark tearing. This will leave a clean stub when the branch is severed.
- Secondly, remove the stub. Start by making a small undercut just outside the branch collar – the bump part where the branch joins the trunk. Make the overcut by angling the cut away from the trunk to produce a slope that sheds rain.
- Always avoid cutting flush to the trunk, as the collar is the tree's natural protective zone where healing takes place.
- If pruning cuts bleed sap, leave them to heal naturally – unless it's a cherry or a plum, in which case apply wound paint.

4 Tidy Up and Tie In Trained Fruit

(mid-November)

OFTEN THE autumn weather is mild and trees respond with a slight growth spurt. Have a good look at all trained fruit – espaliers, cordons, stepovers and fan-trained fruit – and prune out any growth that needs removing if it doesn't conform to the required shape.

Remember that heavily trained fruit is never heavily pruned. If it were, it would promote vigorous regrowth and that would spoil the shape. Most pruning takes place in August, when the growth spurt has slowed, so that any regrowth is subdued and contained (see page 119).

Make sure fan-trained trees are securely tied in and check the stakes and wires of cordons, espaliers, stepovers, etc. If necessary, loosen or replace ties.

Did you know? George Washington (1732–99), the first President of the United States, grew espaliers on his Mount Vernon estate in Virginia and one of his hobbies was pruning his apples. At the time his garden could have rivalled that of any French chateau. It is still in existence and still grows espaliers today.

Organic Tip ✔

Don't apply a winter wash, even a so-called 'organic' mustard-based one. It will kill your predators. When tar-based winter washes became widely used in the 1920s they caused problems with mites (including the apple rust mite) because the predatory mites were also wiped out.

DECEMBER

A cold December is good news for your fruit trees and bushes because it means they will have a good rest. Cooler temperatures will also chill the air and promote good fruit buds, so if it's a cold month you can expect a good fruit crop next year.

Short days allow you to appreciate the silhouettes of your trees and apple and pear pruning is upon us. You can prune in November (see pages 10 and 12), but those in colder districts generally wait until the New Year. Whenever you prune, the weather must be kind, otherwise the frost could penetrate newly pruned wood and kill it, causing die-back.

1 Winter-prune Grapes

(early December)

MOST VINES are sold in pots so they can be planted at any time of year, but they are best planted when dormant (November–March). Don't plant out a very small vine until spring, though, as hard frosts might kill it.

Vines are tolerant of a wide range of soil types, but they must have good drainage. Dig a hole deep and wide enough to take the roots when fully teased out. Double dig and add grit if drainage is a worry.

All vines need support, usually provided by a system of horizontal wires 30cm (12in) apart, beginning 38cm (15in) above the ground – low so that the vine benefits fully from the reflected heat of summer sun.

Vines are rampant plants intent on producing lots of leaves. They should rest between January and March and normally glasshouse grapes are kept as cold as possible at this time of year by opening the doors and ventilators. In April the greenhouse is allowed to get warmer.

If you are using the rod-and-spur system for a vine in a greenhouse or against outside walls (see page 90), after planting cut the vine back to two good buds above the graft point. In spring the best shoot – the 'heir' – is trained vertically to form the main stem. If disaster does not strike, the other shoot – the 'spare' – is cut back to a couple of leaves.

In the second winter the main shoot, or rod, is cut back by about two-thirds to two good buds, as are any laterals – the spurs – so that there is an heir and a spare at each point of the developing structure. You should end up with a main stem with very short (2–5cm/1–2in) branches. In the third and subsequent winters, the rod is reduced by less – about half.

Also at this time of year the rod is untied and the tip is allowed to flop on to the ground. It is usually tied down horizontally in order to slow the sap and keep it away from the apical buds; this will also encourage lateral growth. When the buds begin to break, the rod is tied back into position.

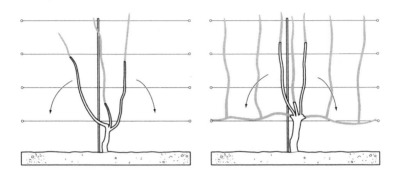

If your grapevine is very mature and rigid, or if it is outside, you may not be able to allow it to flop about. In this case just shorten the laterals as above and secure it well.

If you are growing vines in open ground using the double Guyot system (see page 90), the newly planted vine is again cut down to two good buds above the graft point. One shoot is allowed to develop vertically over the summer and any other shoots are cut back to one leaf. In the second winter the rod is cut back to three good buds at the height of the lowest wire. In the second summer the three shoots are again trained vertically and side shoots reduced to one leaf. In the third winter two of these shoots are cut back to about 75cm (2?ft) long and they are trained along the lowest wire, one to the left and the other to the right. The third is cut right back to three strong buds for next year's replacement shoots. Your vine is now ready and set to produce fruit in its third summer.

Did you know? Tomato food is the best potash-rich food for fruit. It is widely available, but you can make your own high-potash food from 'Bocking 14' comfrey for nothing. Put the chopped leaves into a plastic container with a lid and allow them to rot down to produce a tea. Dilute it one part tea to twenty parts water. The drawback is that the decomposition process smells, although Garden Organic at Ryton use a wall-mounted drainpipe system which contains the stench. The pipe has a removable lid at the top and a tap at the bottom so that the leaves go in the top and the liquid is drained from the bottom.

Organic Tip ✔

A regular watering regime up until the longest day will prevent your grapes from splitting as they ripen. As the fruit forms and colours up, ease off the watering. If growing under glass, do not damp the floor down late in the day as the extra humidity encourages fungal disease.

SECRETS OF SUCCESS

- For further advice on growing grapes, see June, page 90, and August, page 124.

VARIETIES

For varieties of grape, see June, page 92.

2 Check Stored Fruit
(early December)

VERY FEW pears last beyond December, so it will be mostly apples that need checking now. If you have lots of stored fruit it's impossible to unwrap every apple unless you have lots of time. The best course is to check a wrapped sample in each tray or drawer. Gently feel the others, applying gentle pressure, for any signs of softness. If you've laid them out, well spaced, in wooden drawers, a quick glance will tell you if they are keeping well.

Check all your varieties and make sure that you are eating the ones with the shortest storage life first. If you feel that you cannot eat all the fruit that's ready, take some out of store and give it away.

Did you know? Over-ripe apples in store will give out lots of ethylene and this gas will cause other fruit — including later varieties of apple — to ripen precociously. Bruised fruit produces even more ethylene, so make sure you store only perfect apples. A single bruised one can wreak havoc.

Organic Tip ✔

Pick your fruit on the driest days that you can. It will keep for longer. Handle with kid gloves.

3 Tidy and Weed Fruit Cages

(mid-December)

FRUIT CAGES are a godsend: they ensure that you, rather than the birds, get your crop. However, we could get a heavy snowfall this month and the weight of overhead snow could easily bring down your cage or buckle the supports. At best, it will stretch and weaken the netting.

If you possibly can, untie the top, fold it carefully and store it away so that your cage is open to the elements. This will allow the birds access to the ground and they will make short order of eating any pests, including the raspberry beetle which overwinters as a grub.

This is also a good time to weed and tidy the ground under your fruit bushes and canes, as it is likely to have been trodden down every time you harvested. Weeds steal a lot of nutrients, so having a clear fruit patch will ensure that your fruit gets off to a flying start in spring.

Add organic matter now, or feed once the buds begin to break with a nitrogen-rich granular fertilizer. Replace the netting in April.

If you do not have a fruit cage, consider investing in one. The metal-poled ones are expensive – but so is fruit. If you are handy, it is much cheaper to make a wooden one and it will last between 5 and 10 years.

Did you know? Fruit cages seem to be recent arrivals, but in the nineteenth century the invention of barbed wire allowed the owners of cherry grounds to wire-fence their trees. Overhead netting was added to keep off birds.

Organic Tip ✔

Go to a specialist and try to get netting that's large enough for bumblebees to pass through to pollinate. Failing that, lift the sides in spring when much pollination takes place.

INDEX

THE TEN-MINUTE GARDENER

········ THE TEN-MINUTE GARDENER ········→

········ THE TEN-MINUTE GARDENER ··········→

·········· THE TEN-MINUTE GARDENER ···········→

Val Bourne has been a fanatical gardener since the age of five. In her twenties she worked in vegetable research, at a lowly level, and she has always grown her own fruit and vegetables organically. She now has a large allotment, and fruit and vegetable patches amongst her extensive flower garden in the Cotswolds.

An award-winning writer, Val also serves on two RHS panels – dahlias and herbaceous and tender plants, which meet fortnightly to assess plants for the Award of Garden Merit (AGM). She lectures all over the UK and has also lectured in Japan and South Africa. Val writes regularly for the *Daily Telegraph*, *Saga* magazine, *Oxford Times*, *Grow It* and the Hardy Plant Society magazine. She also contributes to the RHS *The Garden*, and *The Rose Magazine*, amongst other publications.

She is the author of six other books, including *The Natural Gardener* (winner of the Gardening Writers' Guild Practical Book of the Year), *The Winter Garden*, *Colour in the Garden* and *Seeds of Wisdom*, as well as *The Ten-Minute Gardener's Vegetable-Growing Diary* and *The Ten-Minute Gardener's Flower-Growing Diary*.

Her passion is still gardening!